Managing Interactive Classroom Learning Communities for Elementary and Middle School Students

Lawrence Lyman
Harvey C. Foyle
Allyson L. Lyman

**DIGITAL TEXT AND FREE PRINTED STUDENT TEXT
NOT FOR RESALE**

The package you have purchased with the CD is a low cost interactive package that included the CD, password protected website and complimentary student printed text. This package, due to its reasonable cost, is not for resale through college bookstores, Amazon.com or any other resale outlets.

Editions are continually updated by adding videos and links and it is unfair to sell outdated material to other students.

Table of Contents

About the Book i

Credits iii

Foreword v

Chapter 1   Teaching Today's Students 1

Chapter 2   Structuring the Interactive Classroom 21

Chapter 3   Managing the Interactive Classroom 45

Chapter 4   Creating the Classroom Community 65

Chapter 5   Maintaining and Enhancing the Classroom Community 87

Chapter 6   Utilizing Collaborative and Cooperative Learning 109

Chapter 7   Activities for Collaborative and Cooperative Learning Lessons 129

Chapter 8   Promoting Active Involvement 155

Chapter 9   Activities to Use Class Time Productively 177

Chapter 10   Becoming the Teacher You Want to Be 205

Afterword 223

Appendix A   Bibliography 225

Appendix B   Chapter Questions 229

Appendix C   Learning Activities 239

Appendix D   Classroom Context Assignment 249

About the Authors 255

About the Book

 Zardozz is an alien who represents the students who have different cultures and languages and may feel as if they are not actively involved and accepted in their elementary or middle school classes. The reader can find Zardozz in various places throughout the book.

 This symbol indicates there is a video clip either embedded in this work or found in an external link. All external video links were working and appropriate at the time of publication.

Text that is bolded, underlined and centered between the left and right margins indicates that there are one or more links to additional information about a topic being discussed. All Internet links were working and appropriate at the time of publication.

Credits
Video and Photo

Video segments and some of the photographs used in this publication were filmed on location at the following sites:

Lowther South Intermediate School
Emporia Unified School District
Emporia, Kansas
Jessica Griffin, Principal
Theresa Davidson, Superintendent
Dr. George Abel,
    Assistant Superintendent for
    Teaching and Learning

Neosho Rapids Elementary School
Southern Lyon County Unified Schools
Neosho Rapids, Kansas
Bill Warner, Principal
Michael Argabright, Superintendent

Olpe Elementary School
Southern Lyon County Unified Schools
Olpe, Kansas
Bill Warner, Principal
Michael Argabright, Superintendent

Ottawa Middle School
Ottawa Unified School District
Ottawa, Kansas
Carmen Schaefer, Principal
David Krumme, Assistant Principal
Dr. Jean McCally, Assistant Superintendent

The Teachers College
Emporia State University
Emporia, Kansas
Dr. Phil Bennett, Dean
Dr. Ken Weaver, Associate Dean
Dr. Marc Childress, Chair
Dr. Jean Morrow, Chair

William Allen White Elementary School
Emporia Unified School District
Emporia, Kansas
Frank Leone, Principal
Theresa Davidson, Superintendent
Dr. George Abel,
    Assistant Superintendent for
    Teaching and Learning

Additional photographs and clip art courtesy of **Pics4Learning.com**

Additional photographs courtesy of **Harvey Foyle** and **Larry Lyman**

Credits
Contributors

Thanks to the following educators who have contributed ideas and material for this publication.

University Faculty and Staff

Tara Azwell	Carlos Galiano	Harriet Johnson
Nancy Smith	Bill Stinson	Sandra Thies

Public School Teachers, Counselors, and Administrators

Jennifer Anderson	Sheila Broyles	Jody Drake
Joanne Foyle	J. D. Horsch	David Krumme
Frank Leone	Darla Long	Susan Lyman
Billie Manderick	Faith Moran	Jo Anne Terrell
Joe Tokarz	Bill Warner	Gwen Wellnitz

Professional Development School Interns

Whitney Czjakowski	Tara Davis	Abraham Marintzer
Brooke Province		Samantha Richmond

Foreword

During my thirty-one year career as an elementary principal, I've had the opportunity to work with dozens of beginning teachers. Fortunately, most of them went on to enjoy productive careers in the classroom. Unfortunately, some of these beginning teachers struggled with classroom management. Many were able to adjust and learn to be effective classroom managers, but those that did not either left education or never became productive and successful classroom teachers.

There were certain competencies that I observed teachers exhibit consistently in well-managed classrooms.

- A consistent and caring approach to classroom management was obvious.

    o Teachers provided a consistent structure throughout the day but realized that, at times, events outside of the classroom needed to be discussed because they impacted the capacity of students to learn.

- Students were treated fairly and equitably, not necessarily equally.

    o All students are unique, and a 'one-size-fits-all' approach will never be successful.

- Classroom rules were posted and developed cooperatively between the teacher and the students.

    o Students respond best when they are active participants in the development of classroom rules rather than having them dictated to them.

- Clearly established classroom routines were evident.

    o Incredible amounts of time can be wasted and multiple off-task behaviors can occur if teachers don't spend sufficient time at the beginning of the year developing and practicing classroom routines.

- A high level of engagement during instruction and a definite academic focus was observed.

    o Teachers need to provide well-planned and developmentally appropriate lessons that follow a logical and sequential pattern.

- Demonstrated smooth transitions between instructional segments.

    o Transitions need to be well planned, orderly, and short. Materials need to be ready to go when needed.

- Provisions were made for early finishers, and differentiated instruction used to allow all students to be successful whatever their ability level.

  o A broad range of student ability levels exist in most classrooms. Teachers need to be aware of that and tailor their instruction to meet their students' needs.

- Opportunities for cooperative learning rather than a totally teacher directed instructional approach were offered.

  o Students thrive with cooperative and collaborative learning. It can be a highly effective instructional technique. Teachers need to spend time early on developing what cooperation and collaboration should look like. Without the appropriate groundwork being developed, chaos can reign.

- Well-established and ongoing communications with parents and/or guardians were in place.

  o Proactive efforts in this area can often prevent problems during the school year. Teachers shouldn't hesitate to share positive developments as well their concerns.

In this book, Dr. Lyman, Dr. Foyle and Ms. Lyman provide the foundations of effective classroom management. This book should be an invaluable teaching tool as they endeavor to prepare the classroom teachers of the future.

Bill Warner, Principal

Neosho Rapids Elementary School
Neosho Rapids, Kansas

Olpe Elementary School
Olpe, Kansas

February 2011

Chapter One
Teaching Today's Students

"I wonder what they *do* teach them at these schools."
Professor Digory Kirke
The Lion, The Witch, and the Wardrobe
C. S. Lewis, Macmillan, 1978, p. 47

Most teachers are concerned about being able to effectively manage their classrooms. This is a valid concern because classroom management is the key to productive student learning, to encouraging positive student attitudes and feelings, and to promoting student interaction which enhances learning. In this chapter, some of the many challenges teachers will face from today's students, from expectations for student success on standardized tests, from changes in technology, and from other factors will be explored.

While teaching today's students and meeting the challenges in today's schools can be a daunting prospect, this chapter will also outline some of the strategies for effectively and efficiently managing the classroom. These ideas and strategies will be the focus of the remaining chapters in the book.

Finally, this chapter will provide some questions for teachers to ask themselves as they work with students. The questions will also provide a focus for thinking about the teacher's own views of his or her ideal classroom and how to create that desirable environment for students using ideas and strategies from this book.

Today's Students

According to the Bureau of the Census, in 2007 there were approximately 74 million children in the United States. Almost 21 million children were under the age of 5.[1] Between 2010 and 2050, the United States is expected to grow *significantly* in racial and ethnic diversity. The proportion of the U.S. population that is classified as non-Hispanic White is expected to decrease.[2]

Today's students are becoming *increasingly diverse* in terms of *socioeconomic status*, *language*, *ethnicity*, and *ability*.[3] The language and culture backgrounds of students in elementary and middle school classrooms will become increasingly diverse. Among the challenges for teachers in diverse classrooms will be: higher incidences of students in *poverty*, lower levels of *parental education*, and higher numbers of students who are *not proficient in English*.[4] The Children's Defense Fund website has additional information on American children.

According to the organization Feeding America, a significant number of children in America live in food-insecure homes. A food insecure home is one without enough nutritious food for the children to eat or without any food at all. For the years 2006-2008, an estimated 18.9 per cent of American children lived in homes that were food insecure.[5]

Mark Rank, Professor of Social Work at Washington University in St. Louis warns that poverty and childhood hunger pose a serious threat to the United States. "If a student is not learning to his full potential, it comes back to haunt us as a society." Rank suggests that failing to ensure that all children have enough nutritional food to eat is "perhaps one of the most foolish things you can do from a policy perspective."[6]

"Give me your tired, your poor,
Your huddled masses yearning to breathe free,
The wretched refuse of your teeming shore.
Send these, the homeless, tempest-tost to me,
I lift my lamp beside the golden door!"

Emma Lazarus

Definition of Classroom Management

Classroom management can be defined as the *decisions* a teacher makes and the *actions* a teacher takes to build and maintain a safe and productive classroom community with the following attributes:

S	Safe and orderly	Rules and procedures are established for the safety and well-being of the students. The teacher actively supervises the students at all times and deals with problems proactively whenever possible.
M	Meets the needs	Both academic and social needs of the students are of the students accommodated.
I	Involvement	Students are actively involved in developmentally appropriate learning activities. Students have frequent opportunities to interact collaboratively and cooperatively with other students. Students are given opportunities to make appropriate choices in the classroom.
L	Learning focused	The teacher makes effective use of the available learning time. Instruction is well planned and appropriate for the curriculum standards and for the learning needs of the students. The teacher helps the students make connections between what the students are learning and their experiences, needs, and interests.
E	Establishes community	The teacher appropriately shares power and ownership of the classroom, rules and procedures, and learning with the students. Mutual respect, problem solving, and conflict management strategies are encouraged.

Although this basic definition of classroom management seems relatively simple and straightforward, classroom management is a complex process which requires careful planning and ongoing reflection on the part of the teacher to insure that the outcomes of the teacher's management decisions and actions are consistent with the teacher's philosophy and belief system.

Classroom management is a *journey*, not a destination. The skills and processes needed to create a classroom community of learners are acquired over time and must be continuously adapted and refined as the teacher works with different groups of students. Teachers who are able to manage their classrooms effectively and efficiently are flexible and open to new strategies and ideas to meet the needs of their students. In one of its Best Practices briefs, Classroom Management, the NEA provides information about Learner Centered Classrooms

The Domains of Classroom Management

Classroom management encompasses four *domains of student learning*. The *cognitive* domain is concerned with the *information and ideas* the teacher hopes the students will acquire. These ideas and information are structured, at least in part, by the curricular standards established by the school district or other governmental agency. The *affective domain* includes *feelings and attitudes* the students have about what they are learning, about their peers, and about their teachers. The *psychomotor domain* focuses on movement and related physical skills. A fourth domain, the *interpersonal domain,* involves interactions students have with others as they are learning.

The Cognitive Domain

The *cognitive domain* often receives the most attention in the classroom. This is due, in part, to the pressure on teachers and students to perform well on required assessments and to meet the demands of local, state, and federal mandates for school improvement. Some of the ways in which the cognitive domain relates to classroom management are:

The Cognitive Domain and Classroom Management

Students understand classroom and school rules and expectations.

Students behave in accordance with school rules and expectations.

Students are engaged in developmentally appropriate learning tasks which are related to their needs, interests, and experiences.

Students have developmentally appropriate roles in the structure and operation of the classroom.

Students can create appropriate solutions to academic and social problems they encounter in the school setting.

Students have opportunities to make developmentally appropriate choices about their learning.

Additional information about the Cognitive Domain
http://www.tecweb.org/eddevel/edtech/blooms.html

The Affective Domain

The *affective domain*, the domain of students' feelings and attitudes, may be the *most important* to classroom management. The attitudes and feelings students have about what they are learning, about their classmates, and about the adults they are working with are often more powerful motivators of student learning than information and ideas. Some of the ways in which the affective domain is related to classroom management are:

The Affective Domain and Classroom Management

Students feel emotionally and physically safe in the classroom and school.

Students feel that their teachers care about them and want them to do well.

Students feel that their peers care about them and that they have friends at school.

Students feel that the school and their classroom work in their best interests.

Students feel that what they are learning is important and useful.

Students feel that they can be successful if they put forth effort to learn.

Additional information about the Affective Domain
http://serc.carleton.edu/NAGTWorkshops/affective/index.html

"Extracurricular Connections in Middle School"

The Psychomotor Domain

They *psychomotor domain*, the domain of physical activities and skills, is also important in classroom management. Some of the ways in which the psychomotor domain is related to classroom management are:

The Psychomotor Domain and Classroom Management

Rules and procedures help students to move around the classroom and school safely and efficiently.

Students have regular opportunities to learn through hands-on learning activities.

Expectations for learning activities, such as seatwork, which require limited movement and concentration, are developmentally appropriate for students.

Students have regular opportunities for physical education activities and for recess.

Additional information about the Psychomotor Domain
http://www.edpsycinteractive.org/topics/behsys/psymtr.html

Additional information about the The Importance of Recess and Getting Children Outside
http://health.msn.com/kids-health/articlepage.aspx?cp-documentid=100244057
http://mrpullen.wordpress.com/2008/01/29/the-importance-of-recess/

The Interpersonal Domain

The *interpersonal domain*, involving interactions between students, is a primary focus of this book. The importance of building a safe and productive classroom community, where students have regular opportunities to work together, cannot be overemphasized. Cooperative learning strategies are some of the best researched and proven ways to help students acquire academic and social knowledge and skills. Some of the ways in which the interpersonal domain is related to classroom management are:

The Interpersonal Domain and Classroom Management

Students have opportunities, structured by the teacher, to get acquainted with their peers and to form friendships.

Students participate in classroom activities, rituals, and celebrations as part of a classroom community of learners.

Students have opportunities to learn and practice communication skills and social skills.

Students have opportunities to work with students who are different from themselves.

Students have opportunities to work collaboratively and cooperatively together on learning tasks and projects.

Students participate in class meetings to plan, share information, and formulate developmentally appropriate group solutions to problems and concerns in the classroom.

Additional information about the Interpersonal Domain
http://pixel.fhda.edu/id/learning_domain.html

"Daniel Goleman's Social and Emotional Learning"

The Importance of Classroom Management

Much is expected of today's teachers. Teachers are being held increasingly accountable for *student achievement*, for *test scores*, and for *accomplishing more with less*. Perhaps the most commonly expressed concern of students, teachers, family members, and administrators is poor classroom management that results in *disruptive student behavior*.[7]

According to the *Los Angeles Times,* "Among the top reasons why teachers are deemed unsuccessful or leave the profession is their inability to effectively manage their classrooms." An analysis by the *Times* indicated that poor classroom management was one of the top reasons why many California teachers had been fired by their school districts.[8]

All teachers need to develop skills and strategies to create a *safe and orderly classroom environment that facilitates learning*. Charles (2002) puts it this way: As a beginning teacher, "you are not going to fail because you have an insufficient knowledge of composition or algebra or world history, nor will you leave teaching because you can't recite the cardinal principles of education or make a lesson plan. If you fail in teaching, it will almost certainly be because you cannot keep students engaged in class lessons."[9]

"A Principal's View, Bill Warner, About Classroom Management"

Challenges in Today's Classrooms

Teachers today are faced with a number of *challenges* as they try to manage their classrooms. The scope and complexity of these challenges can sometimes make a well managed classroom where students are working harmoniously and productively together seem like a dream that is impossible to realize.

- **D** Differences
- **R** Relationships
- **E** Effective teaching strategies
- **A** Assessment and planning
- **M** Meaningful learning activities

Differences in the Classroom

Each student is *unique* in terms of his or her developmental level, the academic and social skills they possess, and the experiences they have had, both in and outside of school. It is a challenging task to structure an appropriate classroom environment and to meet the varied learning needs of each of student. Students are also different in terms of their learning preferences and interests. The ways in which students prefer to learn can affect their achievement and motivation to learn significantly. Such factors as attention span, resourcefulness, responsibility, and perseverance can also vary widely among students.

To work effectively with diverse students, the teacher needs to be able to structure and manage a classroom environment that is responsive to the academic and social needs of students. The teacher must be equitable in dealing with students and provide opportunities for all students to be successful. As Curwin, Mendler, and Mendler noted, "Many children once labeled 'at risk' who grow up to be successful often attribute their success to a caring teacher who took a special interest in them."[10]

Relationships

One of the most important factors in influencing student behavior is the *personal bonds* or *relationships* they have with the teacher and with other students.[11] In the diverse classroom, it is particularly important to help students relate positively to the teacher and to peers by creating a classroom community where students work together peacefully and productively.

Creating *positive, nurturing relationships* with students can be challenging for teachers because of the many things teachers are expected to do each day. This can be especially difficult for the middle school teacher who may interact with 100 or more students each day.

Students who have had negative experiences with adults or with previous schooling may distrust the teacher's efforts to build positive relationships. When children have not related successfully to teachers and peers in the past, they are often resistant at first, even to the most caring teachers. Relationships with these students may require extra attention, time, and effort on the part of the teacher.

Because it is important for the teacher to build positive relationships with students, teachers need to be careful when correcting inappropriate student behavior. This certainly is not to say that inappropriate behavior should not be corrected, but some teachers embarrass or humiliate students as they are correcting their behavior. Strategies for correcting student behavior in appropriate and positive ways will be presented later in this book.

When building relationships with students, it is a good idea for teachers to remember the Golden Rule and to treat students as they themselves would wish to be treated. For example, if a student is behaving inappropriately, taking a moment to correct the student in private is much less likely to embarrass the student in front of his or her peers. This is how teachers would expect to be treated, for example, if they were in a similar situation with their building principal.

Building positive relationships among students also presents challenges for the teacher. Helping children to acquire the social skills necessary to interact harmoniously, to help each other learn, and to share limited resources are important goals for every teacher. Because of limited time and pressures to focus on academics and student achievement, teaching these social and communication skills is sometimes neglected even though these skills are essential to success in schooling and in later life.

Most students are eager for social connections with peers as is evidenced by the California student who sent over 14,000 text messages in a single month. She reports texting a friend who was sitting right beside her at a party. According to a study by Nielson, the 13 to 17 year olds send an average of 1,742 texts per month.[12] Another study by Pew Research Center reports that 43 percent of teens with cell phones report sending at least one text message from a class each day, even though many schools have banned the use of cell phones during class.[13]

Although many students today want to be socially connected to their peers, conflicts among students are still common. Conflict is inevitable whenever groups of people are working together. Bullying is a growing problem in many schools and some students are now victims of cyber bullying as well. An important task of the teacher is to help students get along with their peers by providing opportunities to learn and practice social skills and strategies for managing conflicts with other students.

Relationships with *parents and other family members* can also present challenges for the teacher. Family members can be reluctant to come to school due to time pressures or to negative experiences they had as students themselves. In contrast, some family members are aggressive and demanding of teachers. Teachers need to be willing to welcome family members, to keep them informed, and to address their concerns in a collaborative and caring manner.

In today's schools, teachers must also work together effectively with other staff members to achieve the goals of the school and the community. Today's teachers are usually involved in staff development, cooperative planning, and goal setting which can be time consuming and sometimes frustrating. Working together with other adults in the school, however, is an important factor in the teacher's success.

Effective Teaching Strategies

The teacher's ability to use a variety of *teaching strategies* which are appropriate for the academic and social needs of diverse learners has a powerful effect on student achievement and motivation. When teachers use teaching strategies that actively engage students and promote student success, discipline problems in the classroom usually decrease. Teachers who were working on a grant for the Kansas Department of Education were asked to identify teaching strategies which are effective with students in diverse classrooms.[14] The following list is adapted from their ideas.

Effective Teaching Behaviors for Diverse Classrooms
Identified by Professional Development School Mentor Teachers
Emporia State University – June, 2009

[not necessarily in order of importance]

1. Adjusting lessons to meet the needs of students
2. Choosing materials for teaching that are appropriate to the interests and developmental levels of students
3. Using varied instructional strategies which meet the needs and developmental levels of students
4. Using appropriate and varied assessments which provide formative and summative information about student learning
5. Promoting a safe, non-threatening classroom environment
6. Building positive, professional relationships with students
7. Providing opportunities for all students to be actively involved in learning experiences
8. Giving positive reinforcement and positive feedback equitably to students
9. Providing appropriate opportunities for students to collaborate and cooperate
10. Adapting teaching and assessments to the needs of the students
11. Actively involving students in making rules and solving problems in the classroom
12. Planning reflects preparation for teaching and meeting the needs of all students
13. Celebrating student differences and cultures
14. Observing student and behavior and involvement and adjusting instruction appropriately
15. Using appropriate grading procedures
16. Incorporating different multiple intelligence activities into lesson planning
17. Using learning activities which promote critical and creative thinking
18. Using technology appropriately in planning, teaching, and assessing
19. Communicating positively with parents and family members
20. Working with colleagues to help every student achieve success
21. Reflecting on teaching and making appropriate changes

Assessment and Planning

Planning learning activities to meet the needs of diverse students and *managing a demanding, standards based curriculum* require a great deal of teacher time and energy. Teachers need to be able to plan learning activities which actively engage students, making the best use of available time for teaching and learning. Providing appropriate remediation and enrichment activities by differentiating instruction for students is another challenge facing the teacher. When the teacher plans carefully, instruction usually proceeds more smoothly, helping to minimize problems with student discipline.

One of the most important classroom management skills for a teacher is *time management.* Since the available time for teaching and learning is limited by many factors, careful planning is needed to make the best use of available time. Classroom management can help to structure a classroom environment that is productive and harmonious.

Assessment of student learning is a time consuming process as well. Teachers need to conduct *formative assessments* regularly to determine the level of understanding of the students relative to the objectives the teacher is teaching. These formative assessments provide essential data for the teacher to use in pacing his or her instruction, in selecting instructional strategies, and for sequencing learning activities appropriately.

Summative assessments that sometimes take the form of state assessment tests are often stressful for both students and teachers. The affective domain of classroom management, mentioned earlier, is especially important in helping to encourage students to put forth their best efforts on tests which may seem unimportant to them. When students are part of a community of learners in which they feel valued and liked and when they like their teacher and their peers in return, students may be more receptive to the teacher's requests for them to work to perform well on summative assessments.

Meaningful Learning Activities

Providing learning activities which are *meaningful* for the students is another challenge facing the teacher. As part of the planning and assessment process, teachers need to be able to plan activities which make connections to the student and actively engage the student in learning.

Meaningful Learning Activities

- connected to the students' needs, interests, experiences = *meaningful*

- connected to other learning

- connected to real life

- emotionally engaging

- varied teaching strategies

- appropriate choices

- opportunities for collaboration and cooperation with other students

- opportunities for critical and creative thinking

- opportunities to use literacy skills

Meaningful learning activities form connections between what is being taught and the learners in cognitive, affective, and interactive ways. Such connections are especially important for underachieving students and for those who students who struggle with learning. When learning activities are meaningful to students, there are usually fewer behavior problems in the classroom.

The challenges presented by today's students, by school improvement efforts, by advances in technology and by many other factors sometimes make the dream of successful classroom management seem elusive or unattainable. Obviously, these challenges do cause some teachers to leave the classroom in search of other career opportunities.

While classroom management and teaching are by no means easy, the well prepared, hardworking teacher can use the strategies and ideas about classroom management presented in the following chapters to meet the challenges that have been described and to create a safe and productive classroom community for his or her students. Despite the challenges, there are many good reasons for becoming a teacher today.

"Heart of a Teacher by Paula Fox"

The 'Big Questions' in Today's Classrooms

Four 'big questions" will help to define the effectiveness of your classroom management. These questions can be applied to almost any educational endeavor and relate most directly to the relationships between teachers and their students. The questions are:

The Big Questions

Who cares?
Who says so?
Where can I find out?
How will I use this?

Who Cares?

A familiar aphorism of teaching is "I don't care how much you know until I know how much you care." As previously discussed, the feelings and attitudes of students can have a tremendous effect on their productivity, on their motivation to learn, and on their willingness to work with others.

To structure a caring environment, teachers need to be able to build positive, caring relationships with their students. Opportunities for students to get to know each other and to work together on meaningful learning tasks and projects are important attributes of a classroom community.

Along with the academic skills students are required to master, they need opportunities to acquire communication and social skills for getting along with others. As students work together, they can practice communication and social skills while learning the required academic material. Opportunities to help other students and to serve the school and community can help to enhance a spirit of caring and empathy.

An important goal of parents and teachers is to help children learn to take *responsibility* for themselves and for their actions. This is a crucial requirement for becoming a good citizen, both in and outside the school. When students are part of classroom communities where they experience caring relationships with their teachers and with their peers, they are more likely to learn to be caring and responsible. When asked "who cares", caring and responsible students respond, "I do."

The reader will encounter the concept of *creating a safe and caring classroom community* repeatedly throughout the following chapters of this book. The authors' belief is that the feelings and attitudes of students are of crucial importance to all teaching and learning functions. Teachers who excel at classroom management are able to motivate students by convincing them that they are cared about, that what they do makes a difference, and that they are responsible for the choices they make.

Who Says So?

The classroom is certainly not the only source of information for today's students. They hear rumors, opinions, and facts from family members, peers, television, the internet, and other sources. It is important that students be able to differentiate between what is a rumor, what is someone's opinion, and what may be considered factual information in order to be successful in many present and future roles – as students, as consumers, and as voters, for example.

Some students believe that anything that appears on television or on the Internet is 'real'. They unquestioningly trust the opinions of family members, friends, and even their teachers without questioning the accuracy of the information.

In the classroom, teachers need to help students identify the sources of information in what they are reading and researching. Students need to be able to identify potential bias or prejudice in the points of view of others, as well in their own ideas. For example, when reading a news article, the teacher can help the students identify the sources of the information being presented to determine how reliable the information may be.

Teachers have the responsibility of making sure that students are exposed to different ideas and 'voices', from both primary and secondary sources, to provide fairness and balance in what the students are learning. When working together, students need to learn to actively and respectfully listen to the opinions of other students, even when they may not agree with those opinions. Openness to new ideas and ways of thinking are important qualities of capable learners.

In preparing this book, the authors have included the ideas of a wide variety of educators. These voices include preservice teachers, beginning teachers, veteran teachers, and administrators who will share ideas and model strategies in video segments. Links to a variety of web sites and suggestions for resources for additional reading are also included to present a wide range of support for the ideas being presented and to help the reader consider different points of view.

Teachers will be exposed to a wide range of ideas and strategies for working with students in university classes and in their future school districts. It is important to be able to ask "who says so" as the teacher consider how to make use of the best practices for teaching with students. There is no single 'right' program or strategy to become an effective teacher.

Where Can I Find Out?

To determine "who says so", students and teachers need to learn strategies to research information, to find information from a variety of sources, and to make decisions about the accuracy of the information they are considering. These strategies will include opportunities to discuss information and ideas with peers who can help evaluate the usefulness of the information.

In the future, change is certain. Increases in information and advances in technology will require that students and teachers be able to get information about innovations and changes and analyze their appropriateness and value for their goals and needs.

The world is becoming increasingly interdependent, so it is also important that students and teachers learn to evaluate the impact of events, policies, and changes on the ecology, economics, and well being of living things throughout the world. This process begins in a classroom community where students work together and are respectful of the opinions and ideas of others.

At the end of this chapter and in the following chapters in this book, suggestions for further reading as well as a list of references to some of the information in the chapter are included. These resources and references to help the reader identify the 'voices' the authors of this book used in addition to their own experiences and research. The resources and references are also intended to help the reader find additional information and ideas that may be of interest and help.

How Can I Use This?

Students are more likely to learn and retain information that is connected to their needs, interests, and experiences. Providing meaningful learning activities helps to motivate students to put forth the necessary effort to acquire information and practice needed skills.

Learning can become even more meaningful when it can be connected to the personal goals of students. Teachers can help students set personal goals related to academics, for social skills, and for helping others. When students encounter learning experiences that will help them attain goals they have set, this increases their motivation to learn.

Effective teachers also set personal and professional goals and reflect on their progress toward their goals on a regular basis. In order to meet the challenges posed by today's students and schools, teachers will need to be continuously involved in goal setting, reflection, and celebration when goals are achieved. In the following chapters, you will find many ideas and strategies that can help you set appropriate goals for managing your current or future classroom.

"The 6 Cs: A Framework to Motivate and Engage"

Summary

Classroom management is the process of teachers making informed decisions and taking appropriate actions to build safe and productive classroom communities. Attributes of these safe and productive communities include: an orderly environment, meeting the needs of diverse students, and actively involving students in appropriate learning tasks. Ideally, classroom communities are focused on achieving the curricular goals established by the school district, state, or other regulatory agency while providing opportunities for students to develop positive feelings and attitudes toward learning. Opportunities to learn and practice social and communication skills and to interact with other students are facilitated in effectively managed classrooms.

Today's elementary and middle school students bring many challenges to the classroom. They need teachers who are capable of creating safe and productive classroom communities while helping the students acquire the academic and social skills they will need to be successful in the future. The following chapters will provide strategies, ideas, and resources for effective classroom management.

Additional Resources

Anderson, L. W., & Krathwohl, D. R. (2000). *A Taxonomy for Learning, Teaching, and Assessing: A Revision of Bloom's Taxonomy of Educational Objectives.* Boston: Allyn and Bacon.

Gootman, M. (2008). *The Caring Teacher's Guide to Discipline: Helping Students Learn Self-Control, Responsibility, and Respect, K-6* (3rd ed.). Thousand Oaks, CA: Corwin.

Goleman, D. (2006). *Social Intelligence: The New Science of Human Relationships.* New York, NY: Bantam Dell.

Kohn, A. (2006). *Beyond Discipline: From Compliance to* Community (2nd ed.). Alexandria, VA: Association for Supervision and Curriculum Development.

Levine, D. A. (2009). *Building Caring Classroom Communities: Strategies for Developing a Culture of Caring.* Bloomington, IN: Solution Tree.

VanSlyke-Briggs, K. (2010). *The Nurturing Teacher: Managing the Stress of Caring.* Lanham, MD: Rowman and Littlefield.

Footnotes

[1] U. S. Department of Commerce, Bureau of the Census (2007). 'Child Population 2007'. Retrieved December 9, 2010, from www.census.gov/popest/states/asrh/files/SC-EST-2007-AGE-SEX-RES.csv/.

[2] Ortman, J. M., & Guarneri, C. E. (2009). *United States Population Projections: 2000-2050.* Retrieved December 9, 2010, from www.census.gov/population/www/projections/analytical-document09.pdf.

[3] Morehead, M. A., Lyman, L., & Foyle, H. C. (2009). *Working with Student Teachers: Getting and Giving the Best* (2nd ed.). Lanham, MD: Rowman and Littlefield, p. 83-85.

[4] Goodwin, B., Lefkowits, L, Woempner, C., & Hubbell, E. (2011). *The Future of Schooling: Educating America in 2020.* Bloomington, IN: Solution Tree Press, p. 34-36.

[5] Bauer, L. (2010). Kids Going Without. *Kansas City Star.* December 12, 2010, p. A1, A19.

[6] Bauer, p. A19.

[7] Cangleosi, J. S. (2004). *Classroom Management Strategies: Gaining and Maintain Students' Cooperation* (5th ed.). Hoboken, NJ: Wiley, p. v.

[8] Mehta, S. (December, 2009). *Controlling a Classroom Isn't As Easy as ABC.* Retrieved December 5, 2010, from http://articles.latimes.com/2009/dec/14/local/la-me-classroom-control14-2009dec14.

[9] Charles, C. M. (2002). *Building Classroom Discipline* (7th ed.). Boston: Allyn and Bacon, p. 2.

[10] Curwin, R. L., Mendler, A. N., & Mendler, B. D. (2008). *Discipline with Dignity: New Challenges, New Solutions.* Alexandria, VA: Association for Supervision and Curriculum Development, p. 4.

[11] Mathews, J. (2000). *New Teachers Rarely Learn Classroom Management.* Retrieved December 5, 2010, from www.washingtonpost.com/ac2/wp-dyn/A23017-2000Dec18.html

[12] Inside Edition. (January, 2009). *Teenager Sends 14,528 Tests in a Month!* Retrieved December 5, 2010, from www.insideedition.com/storyprint/2506/teenager-sends-14,528-texts-in-a-month.aspx.

[13] Goldberg, S. (April, 2010). *Many Teens Send 100-Plus Texts a Day, Survey Says.* Retrieved December 5, 2010, from http://articles.cnn.com/2010-04-20/tech/teens.text.messaging_1_text-messaging-cell-phones-teens?=PM:TECH

[14] Morehead, Lyman, & Foyle. p. 97.

Chapter Two
Structuring the Interactive Classroom

"'Pass out the arithmetic books. Please.' On the last word, Mrs. Myers flashed her famous first-day-of-school smile. It was said in the upper grades that Mrs. Myers had never been seen to smile except on the first and the last day of school."

Jesse Aarons in Bridge to Terabithia
Katherine Paterson, HarperCollins, 1987

The Teacher's Philosophical Beliefs

A teacher's *belief structure*, especially in relationship to the philosophy of education, has a major impact on how the classroom learning environment and the children's educational activities are structured.

What do these have in common?

George Bush, former President of the USA
Captain Planet, environmental superhero
Carlisle Cullen, vampire doctor
Joan Jett, rock and roll musician
Scabbers, Ron Weasley's rat
Vincent Van Gogh, artist

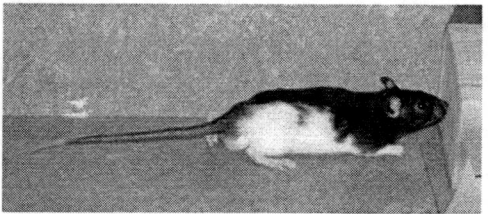

In this example, if the answer is not readily apparent, try this. Underline 'bus' in George Bush. Is the pattern clear? If not, underline 'plane' in Captain Planet. Clear now? If not, one more try. Underline 'car' in Carlisle Cullen. The pattern should be evident – each of the names has a form of transportation in it. It is certainly easier to see the pattern when you know what you are looking for. In the same way, teaching decisions become easier and better when the teacher has a clear sense of purpose and focus – when he or she knows what she is looking for in the classroom environment.

To structure an *interactive classroom* so that the students are *productively engaged* in learning and to manage that classroom, the teacher needs to be sure he or she has a clear, well articulated belief statement or mission statement that provides direction and focus for his or her planning, teaching, assessment, and interactions with students. This belief statement reminds the teacher of what he or she is looking for and guides the processes of decision making and reflection.

Consider the following belief statement:

> The best teaching and learning takes place in a safe and inclusive classroom community where the basic needs of all students are met and students have regular opportunities to interact, to experience academic success, and to experience social success.

This belief statement includes the basic components of the interactive classroom environment that are discussed in this book. The teacher's own belief statement should be used to assist the teacher in making planning, teaching, and assessment decisions that are consistent with his or her beliefs. The belief statement can also help the teacher to be reflective. Based on the belief statement provided, the following questions can be formulated by the teacher to use for evaluating the progress in his or her classroom. While it is important to identify areas for improvement, it is also crucial for the teacher to identify what things in the classroom are going well.

1. Teaching and learning is a process. As a teacher, am I *excited and enthusiastic* about the learning process? Do I try new approaches and ways of doing things? Am I a lifelong learner? What have I learned today?

2. *Safety* is absolutely necessary if students are going to be able to learn. Are my students physically safe? Have I created a classroom community in which students are emotionally safe? Do I interact with students to find out what their concerns and anxieties are? Do I make sure to focus on positive outcomes and avoid sarcasm and humiliation?

3. In my classroom, do students work together as a *community of learners*? Do I share ownership of the classroom with the students? Do I identify and teach social and communication skills so that students can interact effectively with each other? Do I provide regular opportunities for students to work together?

4. Do I meet the *basic needs* of my students? Do all students feel accepted and feel like they belong in my classroom? Do I reinforce the efforts students put forth to learn so they feel competent and successful? Do I give the student reasonable freedom and provide choices consistent with their developmental levels? Is my classroom a fun and enjoyable place to be?

5. Do I utilize learning strategies that encourage *cooperation and collaboration*? Do I provide opportunities for students to work together on projects? Do I encourage critical and creative thinking as students interact? Do I use classroom meetings to provide opportunities for sharing and problem solving?

6. Do I use teaching and assessment strategies that help students to be *successful*? Are students learning the necessary skills prescribed by the curriculum standards? Do I provide activities for enrichment? Do I provide extra help, such as peer tutoring, so that students can be successful? Do I adapt instruction and assessment for the needs of individual students?

7. Do students *interact positively* with each other? Am I aware of students who may feel isolated, left out, and friendless? What do I do to make sure that each student learn to be accepting, compassionate, and empathetic?

What is your belief statement as a teacher? What questions would *you* ask yourself regularly to make sure you are teaching in ways that are consistent with your beliefs? An example of an inspiring belief system can be found at the Coach John Wooden website by clicking on the tab called Pyramid of Success. An excellent question to consider on a regular basis is "If I were a student in the classroom in which I teach, would I be happy and productive?"

SeaWorld and Busch Gardens philosophy of training their animals affirms the importance of a learning environment that is fun, interesting, and stimulating.
http://www.seaworld.org/animal-info/info-books/training/animal-training-philosophy.htm

Begin with a Promise

Teachers sometimes use their belief systems to let students and family members know about their beliefs and goals. At the beginning of the school year, consider what you might say to students and to family members as you begin working together. Some examples are the following ones.

> ### *A Message to Each Student in My Class*
>
> When you come into this class, you can be sure that I'm glad you're here. I'm happy that you are my student. I care about you.
>
> When you come into this class, you have a group of classmates who are your friends. They are ready to work with you and to help you. They care about you.
>
> When you come into this class, you bring talents, skills, and ideas that can make our class a better place to be. I know I can count on you to work with your classmates and to help them. I know you care about us.
>
> We need you and you need us. Let's work, play, laugh, and share together.

Teachers may work together with students to design a promise or pledge for the classroom or school.

> ### *School-Wide Student Standards*
>
> Griffin's Pride
>   Lowther South Intermediate School, Emporia, KS
>   Jessica Griffin, Principal
>
> Participation – being involved
> Respect – caring for yourself, others, and the environment
> Integrity – being honest and responsible for your actions
> Dedication – being a team player and persevering
> Excellence – doing our best and supporting others

"Group PRIDE Activity"

Student Pledge

Lebo Elementary School, Lebo, KS
Darla Long, Principal

Today I will try my best to do my best.
I will listen.
I will follow directions.
I will be honest.
I will respect the rights of other people.
I can learn.
I will learn.

A Promise to Parents

Sheila Broyles, Kindergarten Teacher
Olpe Elementary School, Olpe, KS
Bill Warner, Principal

To my parents:

I promise that I will do my best for your child each and every day. I will do my best to make learning an enjoyable experience. My hope is that your child will learn many things and become a strong problem solver. Some days they will bring it home in their heads and some days in their hands but every day in their hearts.

Create a Physically and Emotionally Safe Classroom Environment

One of the most important factors correlated with an effective school is a *safe and orderly classroom environment*.[1] A safe and orderly environment is one where students feel safe and where expectations are clearly understood and consistent. This safe and orderly environment is correlated with the Effective Schools Research of Ron Edmonds and Larry Lezotte. The Effective schools website provides a wealth of research resources that can be downloaded.

Safe and Orderly Environment

Provide adequate, active supervision of students
Teach and enforce appropriate rules and procedures
Maintain appropriate records
Be aware of student health conditions, medications, allergies
Know about parent custody and other family situations
Observe and appropriately report suspected abuse
Supervise the use of technology
Keep the classroom emotionally safe for students

"Effective School Research"

"Larry Lezotte"

There is no teacher responsibility that is more important that creating a classroom environment that is *physically and emotionally safe* for students (Curwin, Mendler, & Mendler, 2008). Teachers also have responsibility for providing adequate supervision in the classroom, in the hallways, and on the playground to assure the safety of students. Teachers may also be assigned supervision responsibilities such as bus duty or cafeteria duty that also require active supervision of students.

"Creating a Classroom Environment"

To create and maintain the safety of students, the teacher will need to identify *rules and procedures* that promote student safety. These rules and procedures need to be taught as routines to the students and enforced. Students need to be aware of the expectations for their behavior and to know that they are accountable for what they do. Keeping schools safe is an educational priority.

"Rules and Procedures / Classroom Routines"

Every teacher is educationally and legally responsible for providing appropriate supervision of students, especially for 'high risk' activities such as playing on the playground or working with potentially dangerous materials in the classroom. Students should never be left alone in the classroom without adult supervision or placed in the hallway or other place outside of the visual range of the teacher.

Supervision for Playground Safety[2]

1. School-wide rules and procedures for behavior in the hallways, in common areas such as the lunchroom and on the playground need to be understood by the students and enforced by teachers and other school personnel.

2. All rules and procedures, school-wide and in each classroom, should be clear, measureable, and stated in positive terms. ("We keep our hands and feet to ourselves" is preferable to "Don't kick or hit others".)

3. All rules and procedures should be taught, modeled, and practiced with students at the beginning of the school year and to all new students when they arrive.

4. School-wide rules and classroom rules need to be sent home to family members to invite their help in reinforcing these expectations.

5. Positive reinforcement should be used on a regular basis to let students know that good behavior is noticed and appreciated. This is especially important at the beginning of the school year when students are learning and practicing new rules and procedures.

6. Negative reinforcement may need to be used. The most useful negative reinforcement is usually to practice the rule correctly for a time. For example, if the student has been running in the hallway, the teacher would ask the student to walk from a specified destination to another under the supervision of the teacher.

7. Students who cannot conform to rules and procedures may need to be excluded from participation in appropriate activities, especially playground activities, for an appropriate period of time. Parents or guardians would be informed and their support solicited.

8. Anecdotal records are kept by the teacher that note inappropriate behaviors and actions taken by the teacher.

9. Teachers should note the times when safety lessons are taught and when rules and procedures are taught and reviewed in their plan books so that documentation can be provided if needed.

When supervising students on the playground, the teacher should *actively supervise*. This means that the teacher should walk around while supervising rather than visiting with another teacher or engaging in a game or activity with a group of students. The teacher needs to monitor what the students are doing which means the teacher needs to be able to observe the students rather than standing in one place or remaining inside the building during cold weather. If a student is injured on the playground, the teacher needs to send another student for help rather than leaving the playground unattended.

Keeping Anecdotal Records

Teachers have many things to do during each busy day. An anecdotal record can be used to help the teacher remember relevant information about her students. Anecdotal records help the teacher report accurately to parents and to have specific examples to share with parents during conferences. Teachers are also responsible for reporting to administrators, especially about inappropriate student behaviors.

Anecdotal records can also be useful in providing information to other teachers about students. A detailed record about a student with specific examples of behavior is necessary for referral for special education assistance. Students should be aware that anecdotal records are being kept and that they are being held accountable for their behavior by the teacher.

It is important for the teacher to keep a record of inappropriate student behaviors. The teacher should also note incidents of kind and caring behavior, student academic success, student interests, and other relevant information about the student. A file box with index cards, or a notebook with a sheet for each student, is a possibility. Comments made on an anecdotal record should be objective. "A pen was found in Johnny's desk that three students reported was Emma's" is more appropriate than "Johnny stole Emma's pen." If a pattern of such incidents takes place, the record will speak for itself.

The teacher should record any intervention strategies he or she uses with a student as part of the student's anecdotal record (early childhood example). This is very important in early childhood education where a child's behavior is as important as learning content. Examples might be "moved seat", "provided a peer tutor", or "gave the student additional time to finish". This helps the teacher to determine which interventions may be working with a particular student and may be helpful in demonstrating that a variety of strategies have been tried for working with a student.

From time to time, the teacher needs to go through his or her file of anecdotal records and note students with no comments in their record. The teacher can then make a special effort to observe the students and to notice their behavior. This assures that all students are receiving appropriate attention from the teacher.

Other Safety Concerns in the Classroom

Some students come to school with *health conditions* that the teacher needs to monitor. Ultimately, the school board is responsible for formulating appropriate health policies in the school. For example, students may need to take medication at a specified time each day. While many schools provide that the nurse or health aide will administer the medication, the teacher should be aware of what to look for should problems with medication or symptoms of a health problem occur.

Allergies are another kind of health concern that the teacher needs to be aware of. As with medications, allergies are often noted by parents or guardians on the enrollment forms they fill out when registering their child for school. Knowing what to do in case of an allergic attack is important for teachers. The nurse is not always available in an emergency to help.

Legal issues involving *parental custody* of students can also impact the safety of students. Teachers should be aware of legal prohibitions against a parent visiting with a student or removing a student from school. This information is often included with the enrollment forms for a student or may be found in the cumulative record. When questions involving custody of the student occur, the administrator should be consulted.

Teachers are usually designated as mandated reporters of suspected *child abuse*. This legal requirement is another reason why students need to actively interact with all students. Teachers need to be aware of legal requirements for their locale and school district as well as the procedures to be followed in reporting suspected child abuse.

The classroom can also present *hazards* that can threaten the physical safety of students. Some possible classroom hazards include: tripping over classroom furniture, pets in the classroom that may bite, and flammable or dangerous materials. Particularly with younger students, teachers need to check regularly to make sure that the classroom is free of hazards.

Technology, which is increasingly available in the classroom, makes it possible for students to access inappropriate materials on the Internet or to use a classroom computer inappropriately. Diligence on the part of the teacher is needed to assure that technology is used appropriately in the classroom. Rules and procedures for appropriate use of technology need to be established, taught, and enforced at the school and classroom level.

"I'm telling!" or "I'm helping!" Student tattling can reduce student trust and harm relationships among students. Teachers often find tattling frustrating as it can waste valuable instructional time in the classroom.[3] Teachers can help students learn to differentiate between tattling and reporting a dangerous or inappropriate situation to the teacher. Teachers can help students to understand that when the student is "telling" or "tattling", the "teller's" goal is to get attention or to get another student in trouble. When a student is "helping", the student's goal is to inform the teacher of a problem that could threatens the physical or emotional safety of another student. When students come to the teacher to "tell", the teacher helps the student identify their goal by asking "Are you telling or helping?" Obviously, younger students will need considerable practice in identifying their purpose for coming to the teacher. If the student mistakenly identifies a "telling" report as "helping", the teacher can simply say, "You're telling."

As students grow older, there is often a taboo associated with telling the teacher about another student's behavior. However, it is important that the teacher build sufficient trust with students that they will report unsafe behavior, bullying, weapons, or other situations that threaten the physical and emotional safety of others. An extreme example would be students learning of another student planning to bring a gun to school to 'get even' and being reluctant to bring this to the attention of the teacher. While teachers need to reduce incidents of 'telling', teachers still need to actively listen to students when they try to be helpful by reporting situations that the teacher does need to know about.

Emotional Safety

Teachers need to be aware of factors in the classroom that can be perceived by students as threatening to their emotional safety. Students are less productive when they feel threatened or stressed. One theory of how the brain functions suggests that when students perceive that they are threatened, the brain 'downshifts' or processes information on a different level. At these lower levels of processing, the student is less creative and communicates less effectively. When the student is threatened, critical and creative thinking is less likely.[4]

Factors that may cause students to feel *threatened* could include bullying, isolation from other students, overemphasis on grades and achievement, competition, and teacher indifference to students and their feelings. Since evaluation, especially grading, can be threatening to many students, it is important for the teacher to provide opportunities for the students to practice needed knowledge and skills before they are graded. By actively checking for student understanding while teaching, teachers can tell when students are ready to practice a skill independently for a grade. Anxiety can occur when student work is assigned a grade before the student has had adequate opportunities for practice.

Teasing and putdowns can also be perceived as threatening by students. The teacher needs to build the foundation for reducing these threats by avoiding the use of humiliation as a discipline strategy. Sarcasm can also be threatening and reduce trust in the classroom. During the first days of the school year, the teacher needs to emphasize that teasing, putdowns, and other threats to emotional safety are not permitted in the classroom. A poem written by Judith Viorst entitled *The First Day of School* describes some fears that students may have at school. The teacher also needs to monitor the students to assure that such threats are not taking place.

Teachers should also strive to create an environment in which students are willing to take *responsible academic and social risks*. Students need to feel that they can ask questions without being accused of inattention or being made to feel stupid. In an active learning environment, mistakes will naturally occur, and teachers need to reassure students that mistakes can be fixed by working together. Students who are 'at risk' for school failure are particularly vulnerable to threats in the classroom. Factors such as poverty, abuse, learning, or health problems can place students at risk for failing in school.

Suggestions for Working with At-Risk Students[5]

The following suggestions come from an *Adopt-a-Student* program created by Bonnie Lynch and Merle Patterson, administrators at El Dorado, KS Middle School.

1. Make daily eye contact with the students. Students learn avoidance skills early, so breaking down this resistance may take time.
2. Make daily verbal contact with the students. Call the students by name and speak to them whenever you see them.
3. Greet the students by name and tell them goodbye when they leave. Students with attendance problems often respond to being told "I will see you tomorrow."
4. Provide tutoring from the teacher and from peers.
5. Offer a ride home on occasion if you are comfortable with this. Many at-risk students are latch-key students.
6. Encourage students to participate in an extracurricular activity.
7. Attend a school or community activity in which the student participates. Students notice if you support their programs by your attendance.
8. Write praise and success cards for students. Any improvement in attendance, achievement, or attitude should receive recognition.
9. Be aware of student achievement in your class and in other classes. Check with the counselor at downslip time.
10. Show genuine concern. It takes teachers who are very secure in their own self-concept to work with at-risk students.
11. Reinforce success by sharing with other teachers and staff members so they can say "I hear that you ..." Small successes are important.
12. Contact family members with positive comments about their students.
13. Check attendance and office referrals.
14. Pay sincere compliments. Catch students "being good".
15. Give the student a classroom responsibility such as returning books to the media center, passing out papers, taking a message to the office, caring for plants – any short term/no-risk task that is achievable.
16. Give each student 10 minutes one or two times a week.
17. Use cooperative learning strategies. Mixed achievement groups can improve the performance of both at-risk students and students who are not at risk.
18. Visit with the counselor and with other teachers to share ideas about helping students to be successful.
19. Build a supportive and nurturing classroom community.
20. Help each student identify areas of personal strength.

Helping Students Learn to Make Responsible Choices

Helping students to make appropriate choices and to take responsibility for the choices they make is an important goal of teachers. One of the alarming characteristics of contemporary society is the failure of many students as well as adults to take responsibility for their actions. When people blame problems and actions on factors other than themselves, they can be said to be demonstrating an external locus of control. Attributing the cause of unsuccessful efforts to external factors attempts to remove the responsibility from a person and place the responsibility somewhere else.

"Locus of Control"

The teacher's goal should be to help students develop an internal locus of control. People with an internal locus of control are able to take appropriate responsibility for their actions. Teachers can encourage this responsibility by creating a safe classroom environment in which students can make mistakes and take appropriate actions to rectify their mistakes. Teachers also need to model how to take responsibility by demonstrating an internal locus of control when working with students.

"Internal vs External Control and Corporal Punishment"

A few teachers are willing to attribute a student's lack of success to factors outside the teacher's control. Home life, ability, personality, and poverty are examples of factors which can negatively affect student achievement and attitude and are outside of the control of the teacher. The best teachers take responsibility for the factors they can control and continue to help all students to be successful, thus demonstrating the internal locus of control necessary to promote student achievement and success. Teachers' high expectations help to improve student learning.

"Locus of Control – Use It or Lose It by Anthony Dallmann-Jones, founder/director National At-Risk Education Network"

**Examples of
Locus of Control Theory**

External Locus of Control	Internal Locus of Control
Something or someone else is responsible for my behavior.	I am responsible for my behavior and for the choices I make.
I need someone to solve my problems for me.	I have the skills to solve my own problems.
It's not fair!	I treat others fairly and I expect to be treated fairly by others.

Traditional classroom management has emphasized *external* rules and standards. These practices are based on the theory that students are motivated by external forces. In traditional classrooms, when students follow the rules and meet the expectations of the teacher, *rewards* are given. These rewards may include public recognition, extra privileges, good grades, and approval of the teacher. When students do not follow the rules or meet the expectations of the teacher, *punishment* is often used. Punishment may include humiliation, loss of privileges, bad grades, teacher disapproval, or calling the student's parents. These traditional classroom management practices do not encourage students to take develop *internal* motivation to do well. In addition, such practices are often unsuccessful as evidenced by the many students who are not successful and by the prevalence of behavior problems in too many classrooms.

William Glasser offers an alternative theory to explain student behavior that is known as Choice Theory.[6] According to Choice Theory, human behavior can be explained as attempts to meet the *needs* of the individual. Glasser has identified basic needs that motivate all humans, regardless of age or developmental level. Creating a need-fulfilling environment will help students to make appropriate choices, develop responsibility, and achieve success.

"Dr. William Glasser, Reality Therapy & Choice Therapy"

Need Fulfilling Classrooms

Meeting the needs of students helps to create a classroom environment that is safe, nurturing, and productive. According to Alfie Kohn, "…our first question should be "What do students need?' – followed immediately by 'How can we meet those needs?' – and that from this point of departure we will end up in a very different place than if we had begun by asking, 'How do I get students to do what I want?' "[7]

"Alfie Kohn, Too Much Control Over Kids"

Needs of Students

Survival
Acceptance
Power
Freedom
Fun
Feedback
Opportunities for Success

Survival

According to William Glasser, all humans have five basic needs that must be fulfilled in order for people to be secure, happy, and productive. The need for survival is the most basic of all human needs and includes the need for water, air, and food. While teachers cannot control all the factors that influence students outside of the school, a safe and orderly learning environment in the classroom helps to meet this need for students in the school setting.

Glasser's Psychological Needs

ACCEPTANCE. Despite their differences, all people have four basic psychological needs in addition to survival that can be met in a cohesive classroom community.[8] All students need to feel *accepted and to belong*. In the classroom setting, this need is addressed by creating an environment that is emotionally safe for students, free of threats, putdowns, and intimidation. Teachers can help to meet this need by providing group building opportunities for students to get acquainted with each other and to form friendships. Strategies for group building are presented in another chapter. Several ideas, for helping diverse students accept and care for each other, are noted in the Teaching Tolerance Project of the Southern Poverty Law Center.

Helping students work together and to learn and practice social and communication skills helps students to accept each other and to feel as though they belong to a caring community. An example of teaching social skills is the *Words of Wisdom* program developed by the faculty and administration of William Allen White Elementary School in Emporia, KS. The *Words of Wisdom* program incorporates core values common to society that can be taught in the classrooms through student discussions, reading and writing activities, and music activities.

Words of Wisdom
William Allen White Elementary School
Emporia, Kansas
Frank Leone, Principal

September	honesty	courtesy
October	patience	self-control
November	encouragement	appreciation
December	sharing	---------
January	gentleness	kindness
February	cooperation	respect
March	sportsmanship	fairness
April	forgiveness	politeness

POWER. The need for *power*, another basic psychological need identified by Glasser, is addressed when each student becomes a productive part of the group and when the teacher shares power appropriately with the students. Each member of the class must feel that he or she is valued as part of the class and contributes to the success and well being of the class. Some ideas for sharing power with students:

1. Allow students to design and take care of bulletin boards.
2. Display student work in the classroom – every student should have something on display in the classroom at all times.
3. Involve the students in taking care of the classroom environment – equipment, plants, classroom pets.
4. Give the students jobs to do which contribute to the efficiency of the classroom – pass out papers, pick up work areas, make sure lights are turned off.
5. Hold regular class meetings to share ideas and to solve group problems.
6. Nurture support for all students.
7. Involve students in helping to make the rules for the classroom as developmentally appropriate.

FREEDOM. Another basic psychological need of students is *freedom*, according to Glasser. Freedom is supported when respect is shown for individual ideas. Different ways of doing and thinking about things are respected by the students and the teacher. In a classroom where freedom is encouraged, students are allowed to express his or her own unique personality, ideas, and opinions without fear of ridicule as long as they are not harmful or hurtful to others. Students are encouraged to be themselves.

Freedom can be given to students to make appropriate choices regarding their learning activities. For example, students may be given the opportunity to choose the way they would like to demonstrate that they have learned a particular concept or idea.

20 Ways for Students to Demonstrate Their Learning

1. Write questions for other class members to answer.
2. Create a poster, collage, or other visual product.
3. Write and/or produce a play or skit.
4. Design a bulletin board.
5. Participate in a debate or discussion.
6. Create a map, chart, or diagram.
7. Produce a video clip.
8. Make an audio recording of answers instead of writing.
9. Create a hypermedia presentation.
10. Take photographs.
11. Give an oral report in a small group.
12. Write a poem or creative story.

13. Do a demonstration, simulation, or experiment.
14. Write or perform a song
15. Choreograph and/or perform a dance routine.
16. Do a project as part of a team.
17. Make a scale model, exhibit, or diorama.
18. Conduct a survey or poll.
19. Share with a younger group of students.
20. Do research or conduct interviews related to the topic.

FUN. Students also have a basic psychological need for *fun*, according to Glasser. Whenever possible, learning should be enjoyable and fulfilling. As the class engages in learning experiences that are fun and enjoyable, mutual regard is increased and feelings of community are nurtured.

Other Learning Needs – Feedback and Opportunities for Success

FEEDBACK. In addition to the needs identified by Glasser, students also need *feedback* and *opportunities for success* in order to become successful learners. Especially for younger learners, the teacher is the primary source of feedback about his or her learning progress in the classroom. As students mature, feedback from peers can also be useful. Most importantly, students need to learn to evaluate their own learning and to set appropriate goals for improving.

Teachers are well aware that some students succeed easily in the classroom while putting forth minimal effort. Some students need to put forth significantly more effort than their peers and often achieve less for this effort. Teacher feedback helps students to aware of the progress that they are making and to know that students will know that the teacher recognizes and appreciates their effort.

Teachers can encourage student persistence by emphasizing their *progress*. Because learning often takes place in small, incremental steps, students can become discouraged with the time it takes to master a difficult skill or concept. By providing feedback that tells the student his or her effort is producing observable progress and by encouraging appropriate peer and self-evaluation, the teacher can reassure the student that effort will pay off. It is important to provide regular feedback when a student is trying to improve a skill or to change an undesirable behavior.

When providing feedback to students, teachers need to provide an *appropriate amount* of feedback. Too much or too little feedback will limit the effectiveness of the information. One specific suggestion for improvement is usually appropriate for a single performance. Noticing one or two positive attributes of a student's work help the student to know how to replicate what he or she did well with future learning tasks.

Feedback should help the student to *understand specifically* what made his or her effort successful or specifically what the student can do to improve. The student needs to understand what to do more of or what to do less of in the future. It is usually desirable to emphasize the positive elements of the work.

Teachers can use a number of strategies to provide feedback to students about their effort and accomplishments. Comments on student papers, verbal feedback from the teacher, nonverbal signals of approval or disapproval, rubrics, and checklists can provide feedback to students. An important goal is to help the student learn to evaluate his or her own effort and progress accurately.

SUCCESS. In order for students to be successful, they must put forth *effort* to learn. According to Hunter and Barker[9], the student must be able to succeed if he or she does, in fact, put forth effort to learn. Feedback from the teacher is needed so that students learn that their effort, not natural ability or luck, is the key to his or her success in the classroom.

Beginning teachers often say that they want to treat all students equally. To help each student become successful, however, it is necessary to treat students *equitably*. Equal treatment of students implies a "one size fits all" approach to teaching, planning, and managing the classroom. Equitable treatment assures that each student is provided with regular opportunities for success in the classroom.[10]

Teachers who strive to treat all students equitably will want to make sure that all students have regular opportunities for positive interactions with the teacher. Keeping a tally of positive interactions with the student on a seating chart, for example, can help the teacher assure that all students are getting at least one positive interaction per day with the teacher.

Teachers can help to motivate students through classroom instruction. Jere Brophy provides a synthesis of motivation strategies. Learning activities, teaching strategies, and assessments should be structured and organized to provide equitable opportunities for both academic and social success. Teachers can help students to be successful by using a variety of learning strategies and by making appropriate adaptations to the curriculum to accommodate the wide range of ability levels and interests in the typical classroom.[11]

The frustration experienced by a student who has difficulty achieving success in the classroom is expressed in the poem, *My Teacher Doesn't Understand Me* by Jo Anne Terrell[12]. Some *Suggestions for Ways to Help Students to Feel Successful*[13] can help alleviate the issue of frustration and failure. There are many examples of famous people who experienced difficulty in school but did not give up.

Recording Chart for Success for All Students

Use some of the suggestions given to make each student in your class feel successful at least three times during one week. Use the seating chart to fill in each student's name, and then make a tally mark each day he or she has an opportunity for success. Each student should have three marks by Friday.

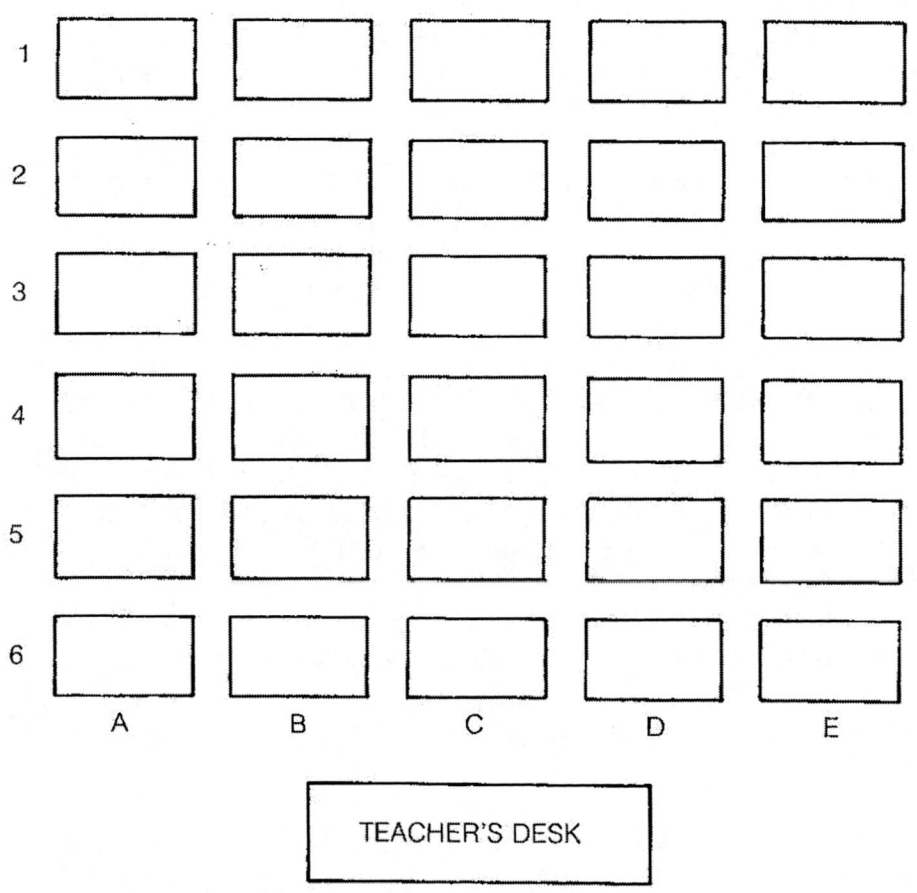

Suggestions for Designing Learning Activities for Student Success

1. Learning activities should be at the appropriate instructional level so that each student can succeed if he or she puts forth effort to learn.

2. Activities should be related to the experiences and interests of students whenever possible.

3. Students should be actively involved and engaged in the learning process.

4. The teacher should provide prompt, specific feedback to students that recognizes student progress and effort.

5. The teacher should check for student understanding consistently so that students do not become frustrated or confused.

6. Students should have opportunities to practice needed skills and concepts before being graded on their performance.

7. Group building activities should be used to help students practice social and communication skills and to provide structured experiences in working with others.

Summary

Student interaction can flourish in a safe, nurturing, and productive classroom environment. The teacher's philosophical beliefs and willingness to evaluate his or her own teaching practices, making changes and adjustments as needed, help to create the structure required to build the classroom community necessary to create and sustain such an environment. Perhaps the most important task of any teacher is to create a classroom environment that is both physically and emotionally safe for students. All students need to feel secure and safe, but this need is especially important for at-risk students who may have been unsuccessful in other school settings.

Structuring the classroom so that the needs of students are met can help students to learn to make responsible choices, to solve problems, and to achieve academic and social success. Utilizing a variety of developmentally appropriate learning strategies and adapting the curriculum to the needs and interests of the students promotes positive interaction among students and encourages student engagement in learning.

Additional Resources

Blanchard, K., et. al., (2002). *Whale Done! The Power of Positive Relationships.* New York, NY: Simon and Schuster.

Bluestein, J. (2001). *Creating Emotionally Safe Schools: A Guide for Educators and Parents.* Deerfield Beach, FL: Health Communications.

Cangelosi, J. S. (2007). *Classroom Management Strategies: Gaining and Maintaining Students' Cooperation* (6th ed.). Hoboken, NJ: Wiley.

Curwin, R. L., Mendler, A. N., & Mendler, B. D. (2008). *Discipline with Dignity: New Challenges, New Solutions.* Alexandria, VA: Association for Supervision and Curriculum Development.

Glasser, W. (1998). *Choice Theory: A New Psychology of Personal Freedom.* New York, NY: HarperCollins.

Ginsberg, M. B., & Wlodkowski, R. J. (2000). *Creating Highly Motivating Classrooms for all Students: A Schoolwide Approach to Powerful Teaching with Diverse Learners.* San Francisco, CA: Jossey-Bass.

Larrivee, B. (2009). *Authentic Classroom Management: Creating a Learning Community and Building Reflective Practice* (3rd ed.). Upper Saddle River, NJ: Pearson.

Springer, S., & Alexander, B. (2005). *The Organized Teacher: A Hands-On Guide to Setting and Running a Terrific Classroom.* New York, NY: McGraw Hill.

Thompson, J. G. (2009). *The First-Year Teacher's Checklist: A Quick Reference for Classroom Success.* San Francisco. CA: Jossey-Bass.

Wong, H. K., & Wong, R. T. (2009). *The First Days of School: How to be an Effective Teacher.* Mountain View, CA: Harry K. Wong Publications.

Footnotes

1. Edmonds, R., & Lezotte, L. (1982). *The Correlates of School Effectiveness.* Arlington, VA: Educational Research Service, Inc. Iowa Association of School Boards. (1987). *Recommendations for a Productive School Model with Strategies for Achieving the Model.* Des Moines: Iowa Association of School Boards. Lezotte, L. (1992). *Creating the Total Quality Effective School.* Okemos, MI: Effective Schools Products, Ltd.

2. Lyman, L., Wilson, A. P., Garhart, C. K, Heim, M. O., & Winn, W. O. (1987). *Clinical Instruction and Supervision for Accountability* (2nd ed.). Dubuque, IA: Kendall/Hunt.

3. Nelsen, J., et.al. (1996). *Positive Discipline: A Teacher's A-Z Guide.* Rocklin, CA: Prima Publishing, p. 322-324.

4. Hart, L. A. (1981). The Three-Brain Concept and the Classroom. *Phi Delta Kappa.* March, 1981. P. 504-506.

5. Lyman, L., & Foyle, H. C. (1990). *Cooperative Grouping for Interactive Learning: Students, Teachers, and Administrators.* Washington, DC: National Education Association, p. 36.

6. Glasser, W. (1988). *Choice Theory in the Classroom.* New York: Harper Perennial.

7. Kohn, A. (1996). *Beyond Discipline: From Compliance to Community.* Alexandria, VA: Association for Supervision and Curriculum Development, p. xv.

8. Glasser, W. (1988). p. 26-34.

9. Hunter, M.. & Barker, G. (1987). If at First You Don't Succeed … Attribution Theory in the Classroom. *Educational Leadership*, October, 1987, p. 50-53.

10. Morehead, M. A., Lyman, L., & Foyle, H. C. (2009). *Working with Student Teachers: Getting and Giving the Best* (2nd ed.). Latham, MD: Rowman and Littlefield. p. 85-86.

[11] Deschanes, C. Ebeling, D. G., & Sprague, J. (1994). *Adapting Curriculum and Instruction for Inclusive Classrooms: A Teacher's Desk Reference.* Bloomington, IN: Institute for the Study of Developmental Disabilities, p. 13-15.

[12] Terrell, J. in Lyman and Foyle (1990), p. 56.

[13] Lyman, L. and Foyle, H. C. (1990). 50-54.

Chapter Three
Managing the Interactive Classroom

In this classroom
Everyone is a student
Everyone is a teacher

First Year Letters
Julie Danneberg and Judy Love
Charlesbridge, 2003

Clear and Consistent Expectations

Clear and consistent *expectations* help to create a safe and need-fulfilling classroom environment. Appropriate rules and procedures help the students understand what is expected and provide guidelines for behavior. In a classroom where rules and procedures are clear, consistent, and reasonable, students will tend to feel safer. Establishing rules and procedures is especially important in the interactive classroom where students will be moving about, interacting with others, and making responsible choices.

The 'WE PUMP' strategy can be used to formulate rules and procedures and to teach these rules and procedures to the students.

WE PUMP

W	Welfare or safety of the students
E	Efficiency
P	Purpose of the rule or procedure is clear to the students
U	The students Understand the rule or procedure.
M	The teacher has Modeled the rule or procedure with the students
P	The teacher provides appropriate Practice for the rule or procedure

Rules and procedures should have a clear and definite *purpose*. Rules should be related to the welfare or safety of the students. Procedures are designed to help make the most efficient use of the time and resources. For example, following recess on a hot day, most students might want a drink from the classroom drinking fountain. An appropriate procedure for using the drinking fountain would help to shorten the time the students take to get their drinks and would make sure that each student gets a drink if they want one.

At the beginning of the year, the teacher will usually involve students by letting them suggest ideas for appropriate rules. Students may also suggest procedures that would be useful helping things to run smoothly in the classroom. While the teacher can invite student input, he or she needs to help the students refine and edit their ideas so that the expectations agreed upon are clear and are consistent with the teacher's goals and belief system. The teacher also retains responsibility for making sure that the rules and procedures are consistent with the school rules and expectations and for making sure the administrator and family members are informed of the rules and procedures. The teacher may choose to post the rules on a sheet of poster paper so that all students can sign that they agree to follow the rules of the classroom.

Suggestions for Creating Appropriate Classroom Rules

1. Simple, clear language

2. Rules should be phrased positively. (what to do, not what not to do)

3. Developmentally appropriate for the students

4. Five or fewer rules (Procedures will also be necessary.)

5. Classroom rules should be consistent with school-wide rules and procedures.

6. Do not specify consequences for violating the rules.

7. Inform your administrator and family members of the rules you have chosen. Be sure to have a way for family members of students who enroll after the first week of school to get this information.

8. Have students commit to follow the rules by having them sign a class poster with the rules or having them sign an individual copy.

In the Star Classroom, for example, four student behavior components are prevalent: **S**afety first, **T**ry your best, **A**ccept responsibility for what you do, and **R**espect people and property. When students practice these four behaviors, the classroom starts being a positive learning environment.

The Star Classroom
Example of Classroom Rules

Safety first   **Try your best**

Accept responsibility for what you do   **Respect people and property**

Procedures are designed by the teacher in accordance with his or her needs and the needs of the students. For example, the teacher may determine that before school begins each day, he or she needs time to check with individual students and finish getting things set up for the day to go smoothly. The teacher could create a procedure for students to come into the classroom, take care of routines like choosing hot or cold lunch, and get productively involved with the help of student monitors. Obviously, procedures have to be suited to abilities and developmental levels of the students.

Some Procedures to Consider

Within the classroom
1. Entering and leaving the classroom
2. Monitor jobs and duties
3. Seating
4. Attendance and lunch count
5. Transitions between activities
6. Using classroom equipment (computers, drinking fountain, pencil sharpener)
7. Using the rest room
8. Keeping the classroom clean and orderly
9. Class discussions
10. Bringing cell phones, money, toys, and other items to school
11. How to turn in assignments and homework
12. Signal for stopping and paying attention to the teacher

Outside the classroom (may be covered by school-wide rules and procedures)
1. Arrival and departure at school
2. Fire drills, tornado drills, crisis plan
3. Lunchroom
4. Hallways
5. Injury and illness
6. Going to other classrooms (music, physical education, art)
7. Appropriate and safe use of playground equipment
8. Using the phone in the office

Signals

A procedure, which is very important in the classroom, is a *signal* for stopping and paying attention to the teacher. This procedure is used so that the teacher can get student attention quickly in case of an emergency, so that instructional time is used efficiently, and so that the teacher does not need to raise his or her voice or become frustrated when student attention is needed. An effective signal is to have the students raise their hand when they see the teacher raise his or her hand. Like other rules and procedures, the attention signal needs to be modeled and practiced so that students will learn to respond to it. Some ideas for using signals for quiet can be found at the Responsive Classroom.

Attention Signal

When you see the signal →
    Put your hand up
        Stop talking
            Stop moving around
                Put anything in your hands down
                    Pay attention to the teacher

Teaching Rules and Procedures

To teach the rules and procedures at the start of the school year, the teacher helps the students *understand* the purpose of each rule or procedure. This is usually simple – the rule helps us to be safe and the procedure helps us to get things done. When students understand that rules and procedures are designed to make the classroom environment safe and productive, they are usually more willing to conform to these expectations. When teaching rules and procedures, the teacher should make sure students understand the rule or procedure. For example, if the expectation is that students will not talk in the hall, the teacher needs to make sure the students understand that no talking is expected, not quiet talking or whispering.

Modeling is another component of teaching rules and procedures to students. When modeling the rule or procedure, the teacher has students demonstrate examples of appropriate conduct. For example, the teacher may ask the students to show what to do when the teacher gives the signal for attention. As discussed earlier in this chapter, the playground can provide particular challenges for keeping students safe, so it may be productive for the teacher to spend the first recess period together having students model the correct use of the available playground equipment. The Responsive Classroom has additional suggestions for interactive modeling.

"Line Procedures – Sheila Broyles"

During the first week of school, students need many opportunities to *practice* the rules and procedures with feedback from the teacher. As the students line up for lunch, for example, the teacher can give positive reinforcement if the students have lined up properly. If the students don't do what is expected, the teacher can provide additional opportunities for practice – not as punishment, but as an opportunity for the students to learn and demonstrate the expected behavior.

As the school year progresses, rules and procedures may need to be reviewed and taught again. When most of the students are having trouble with a rule or procedure, modeling and practicing should be part of the review. If individuals are having trouble with a particular rule or procedure, an effective consequence is to have the student practice the rule several times correctly while the teacher observes.

A caring classroom depends on the *tone* set by the teacher as he or she interacts with the students. At the beginning of the school year, as the students are learning about the teacher's expectations and participating in group building activities, it is especially important for teachers to give a large amount of positive reinforcement to encourage the behaviors and attitudes the teacher wants to nurture. Using *positive reinforcement* on a regular basis throughout the school year contributes to a positive classroom climate and allows the students to know that the teacher notices and appreciates their efforts. The 4-H Clubs promote positive reinforcement by using statements from 100 Ways to Say Very Good.

Positive Strategies for Dealing with Misbehavior

Creating a safe, need-fulfilling classroom with clear expectations that are positively reinforced by the teacher will help to *prevent* a great deal of student misbehavior. Using group building strategies to build a classroom community, discussed in the following chapter, will also encourage positive behavior and attitudes. These efforts, however, will not prevent all misbehavior from occurring in the classroom.

According to Curwin, Mendler, and Mendler (2008), in a typical classroom, approximately 80 per cent of the students don't really need a discipline plan since they rarely break the rules. For approximately 15 per cent of the students, clear expectations and consequences are necessary since these students will break the rules occasionally. Approximately 5 per cent of the students are chronic rule breakers. Successful teachers are able to plan for the needs of all three groups of students.[1]

When *minor behavior* occurs in the classroom, there are some general strategies that the teacher can use to deal with the misbehavior in positive and productive ways. Examples of minor misbehavior include: talking when the teacher is speaking, being out of his or her seat without permission, not completing work on time, not making appropriate use of work time, socializing with other students during work time.

> **Dealing with Minor Misbehavior Positively and Productively**
>
> Reinforce the students when they are acting appropriately
> Use positive reinforcement, positive feedback, and extinction as much as possible
> Reinforce effort by students to improve
> Allow time for interventions to work
> When minor misbehavior stops, use positive reinforcement or feedback
> Don't do anything to a student you wouldn't want done to you

When dealing with student misbehavior, it is important to keep in mind a principle adapted from the *Golden Rule*: don't do something to a student you would not want done to yourself. Writing a misbehaving student's name on the board, humiliating the student, threatening the student, and using sarcasm are examples of strategies teachers would not like to be subjected to themselves. Therefore, teachers should make every effort to correct inappropriate behavior in positive ways that do not harm the self-esteem of the student.

> **Strategies for Dealing with Minor Misbehavior**
>
> Review rules and procedures
> Ignore the misbehavior
> Redirect the student
> Positively reinforce appropriate behavior when it occurs
> Use group alerting procedures and appropriate interventions

At the beginning of the school year, students may misbehave because they do not *remember or understand* a rule or procedure. This may also be true when students have been out of school for an extended period of time such as winter break. New students joining the class after the school year has begun may also be confused about expectations. The teacher can review the rules or procedures not being followed by having a class discussion or class meeting. It may be appropriate to have students role play examples of following the rule and examples of not following the rule. It is important to review the purpose of the rule and procedure. After reviewing the rules and procedures as necessary, the teacher should especially notice when students are behaving correctly and reinforce individuals or groups as appropriate.

Extinction

Sometimes the best response to an inappropriate behavior is to *do nothing*. This deliberate ignoring of misbehavior is also called extinction. One of the most common reasons for inappropriate comments or actions in the classroom is to get the attention of the teacher or classmates. For example, the student may make an off task response to a teacher's question with the goal of making his peers laugh. If the teacher responds to the student, even negatively, he or she has provided the attention the student wanted and the student is likely to try this approach again.

Another example in which ignoring the behavior might be an appropriate choice is when the teacher has asked the students to raise their hands before responding and one student blurts out an answer without raising her hand. It is hard for many teachers to ignore a student who responds in this manner, especially if her answer is correct. By ignoring the response and calling on a student who has his or her hand raised as instructed, the teacher reinforces the expected behavior. If the blurting student then chooses to raise her hand for another question, it is important that the teacher positively reinforce this effort by giving her a chance to respond. It may be effective to provide positive feedback, "Amy, thank you for raising your hand" before the student answers.

"Classroom Management Strategy – Extinction"

Positive Reinforcement and Feedback

Positive *reinforcement* and positive *feedback* are powerful ways for the teacher to encourage appropriate student behavior. This approach is sometimes called "catch 'em being good". For the student seeking attention, for example, the teacher would reinforce the student when he or she is behaving appropriately and not seeking attention. Appropriate positive reinforcement and feedback involve both *verbal* and *nonverbal* language from the teacher. As you view the video examples of positive reinforcement and positive feedback that follow, watch the teacher's body language as you listen to his or her reinforcement or feedback.

Positive reinforcement occurs when the teacher recognizes an appropriate behavior, response, or effort with a positive phrase such as "awesome", "good job", or "just right". Positive feedback is more powerful because it pairs the reinforcement with what the student did that was correct or appropriate. "You are sitting quietly so you may line up" and "Your answer was a great example of a simile" are statements that let the student know what he or she did that was appropriate. Comments on student papers can also provide this positive feedback by letting students know what was positive about their work on a specific assignment. For a student's creative writing assignment, for example, the teacher might write "Great story. Tell me more about …"

"Classroom Management Strategy – Positive Reinforcement in Kindergarten"

Classroom Management Strategy – Positive Reinforcement in Fifth Grade

Classroom Management Strategy – Positive Reinforcement in Sixth Grade

"Classroom Management Strategy – Positive Feedback in Fifth Grade"

Group Alerting Procedures and Interventions

The teacher may need to use appropriate *group alerting* procedures and *interventions* to correct inappropriate behavior when students do not respond to more positive approaches. Whenever possible, interventions need to leave the student in control – that is, group alerting and interventions should encourage the student to make appropriate behavior choices. For example, the teacher may encourage the students to stay on task by reminding them that they have a limited amount of time to finish their work. If a student has not made appropriate use of the work time provided by the teacher to finish an assignment the student was capable of finishing, the teacher may intervene by telling the student that he cannot go outside for recess until the assignment is finished. When the student has demonstrated the appropriate behavior, finishing the assignment, the consequence is removed and he can go outside for recess. The student's *effort* to correct the behavior has a positive result, so the responsible behavior is more likely to reoccur.

Examples of Group Alerting Procedures

Signals
Countdown
Timer
Schedule Posted on Marker Board or Smart Board

Since efficient use of the time available for teaching and learning is a priority, *group alerting procedures* can help students manage their time effectively and motivate students to work harder when time is limited. Group alerting procedures are especially effective with older elementary students and middle school students who usually have a better concept of time.

Signals are useful to check for student involvement and understanding. In the following video example, the teacher asks the students to put their thumbs up to show they understand. This kind of signal is also called an *every pupil response.* Different strategies for every pupil responses are discussed in chapter 8. This group alerting procedure lets students know their involvement is being monitored by the teacher.

"Classroom Management Strategy – Thumbs Up Signal"

Signals can also be used to let students know that their behavior or response is inappropriate. In the following video example, the teacher uses nonverbal signals to let the students know what they should be doing.

"Classroom Management Strategy – Wait Time Signal"

"Classroom Management Strategy – Nonverbal Signal"

A *countdown* is a group alerting procedure that is useful in making transitions from one activity to another or to get the group's attention. When the countdown is completed, the students are expected to be ready to listen and participate in the activity. As was discussed earlier in this chapter, it is useful to have a commonly used *attention signal* to have the students stop their work and look at the teacher.

"Classroom Management Strategy – Countdown"

A *timer* can be used to signal the students to get ready to make a transition to a different activity or to plan so they can finish a given task in the remaining time. In the following example, the teacher uses a timer on the smart board and an oral reminder to let the students know how much time they have left to work.

"Classroom Management Strategy – Timer"

Another group alerting procedure is to *write the schedule* on the marker board or smart board. For example, if the students are working on a language arts activity from 9:00-9:30 and beginning math at 9:35, posting this information lets the students know how much time they have to work before making a transition to the next activity.

> **Examples of Interventions**
>
> Proximity
> Desists
> Private reminder
> Make a plan

Proximity

Proximity to the student can affect his or her behavior. If a student is off task, for example, the teacher may decide to move closer to the student as he or she is teaching. This proximity will often cause the student to pay attention to the lesson. It is a good idea to move around while teaching, if possible, so that the teacher is in proximity to all students at times.

If a teacher notices a student looking inside his desk when he is supposed to be listening to the teacher's presentation, the teacher may not be able to physically move to be in proximity to the student. It is also effective to call on a student sitting near the student who is off-task to respond to a question. Since students' attention will usually move to the student who is answering, the off-task student may begin to pay attention.

"Classroom Management Strategy – Proximity in Third/Fourth Grade"

"Classroom Management Strategy – Proximity in Fifth Grade"

Desists

Desists are interventions by the teacher that are designed to stop inappropriate behavior and help the student to demonstrate the desired behavior instead. Examples of desists include *redirecting, postponing*, and *using I-messages*.

Redirecting a student who is choosing an inappropriate activity or behavior is another way to deal with misbehavior in a positive way. To redirect, the teacher tells the student what he or she should be doing instead. The teacher may provide a choice. If two students are visiting together in the reading corner instead of reading, for example, it may be appropriate to ask, "Would you like to read your book at your desk or at the table in the front of the room?" Older children may be appropriately redirected by asking the student "what should you be doing now"? In the following video example, the teacher redirects the student nonverbally without interrupting the smoothness of his lesson or calling attention to the student.

"Classroom Management Strategy – Postponement"

Another example of a desist is for the teacher to *postpone* acting on the behavior until a later time. If the student shares information that is off-task, for example, the teacher could say to the student, "We won't take class time for that now. We can talk about it later."[2] The student remains in control because he or she determines whether to seek the teacher out to talk about it later.

Some students want to engage in a power struggle with the teacher. The teacher may be able to defuse the power struggle by telling the student that, "I will visit with you later when I am not so angry." This lets the student know that the teacher is making an effort not to respond in anger to the student. The discussion can be *postponed* until a later time when the student's "audience", his or her peers, are not watching the interaction.

An *I-message* can be a helpful desist to let the student know what the effects of his or her misbehavior are. I-messages invite cooperation from the student while reinforcing the appropriate behavior that the teacher expects. There are three parts to an I-message.

Components of an I-message

Describe the inappropriate behavior.	"When you talk while I am giving directions,"
Tell the effects of the behavior	"You and the students around you miss important information."
Make a reasonable request	"Would you please pay attention?"

Private Reminder

A *private reminder* is another intervention that may work with some students. The teacher helps the student remember the appropriate behavior while he or she is in proximity to the student. The teacher may ask the student a question such as, "What do you need to be doing now?" to help the student remember what he or she is supposed to be doing.

Effective interventions should be followed up by appropriate positive reinforcement or positive feedback when the student makes an effort to improve his or her behavior. The teacher needs to let the student know that he or she recognizes and appreciates the student's effort to behave appropriately.

Make a Plan

The teacher can *make a plan.* When the teacher works with a student on the plan, he or she should remember Barbara Coloroso's six critical life messages: (1) I believe in you, (2) I trust in you, (3) I know you can handle this, (4) You're listened to, (5) You're cared for, and (6) You're very important to me. Working with the student, the teacher formulates a plan for changing the inappropriate behavior. The plan should leave the student in control.

"Six Critical Life Messages"

When making a plan, the teacher and student may agree on a reward if the plan is followed. A consequence for not following the plan may also be part of the plan with the student. When the plan is completed, the student needs to commit to following the plan that has been agreed upon. If the plan does not work or the student does not follow the plan, a new plan can be formed.

Consequences for Misbehavior

At times, it may be appropriate for the teacher to impose a consequence for the student's misbehavior. It is important to note that consequences are not "one size fits all". What may be a devastating consequence to one student can be meaningless to the next. The teacher should be aware of the students' personalities, students' developmental characteristics, and family expectations and make any consequence is appropriate for the needs of the individual student or students involved. According to Barbara Coloroso, consequences need to be Reasonable, Simple, Valuable, and Practical (R.S.V.P.)[3] Several handouts can be found at kids are worth it!

"Barbara Coloroso Normalizes the Frustrations of Parenting"

Chronic Misbehavior

When misbehavior reoccurs despite the teacher's efforts, the teacher should analyze his or her own behavior to determine if the teacher is inadvertently contributing to the misbehavior. Some questions to consider:

1. Are my expectations for student behavior clear and consistent?

2. How are the student's needs for acceptance, power, freedom, fun, feedback, and success being met in your classroom?

3. Are your expectations for the student's behavior realistic for the cognitive and developmental levels of the student?

4. Do you practice ignoring inappropriate behavior whenever possible when the student makes inappropriate demands for attention or displays other inappropriate behavior?

5. Do you help the student to experience success academically and socially?

6. Do you provide attention, positive reinforcement, and positive feedback to the student when he or she is behaving appropriately?

7. Have you asked colleagues for information about the student and for suggestions about working with the student?

Serious Misbehavior

Serious misbehavior threatens the safety or well being of the students or the teacher. Violence, both physical and emotional, is an example of serious misbehavior. Other serious misbehaviors include damage to property, vandalism, and defiance of the teacher. Chronic misbehavior may sometimes be defiance – the student telling the teacher "you can't make me behave". Whenever serious misbehavior occurs, the teacher needs to be sure that the administrator is notified about what happened, who was present, and what actions were taken by the teacher.

William Glasser's Reality Therapy model is a helpful way to engage in problem solving with the student to determine a plan to correct the misbehavior. To use the Reality Therapy model, the teacher needs to be committed to changing the way he or she is working with the student.

"William Glasser's *Reality Therapy* Model"

For Reality Therapy to be effective, the teacher needs to be positively and constructively involved with the student. To change chronic misbehavior, for example, the teacher may need to give the students two minutes of positive attention, not related to behavior, every day for ten days.

Reality Therapy strategies, found at the William Glasser Institute, help the teacher to formulate a plan with the student to change or correct the inappropriate behavior. (On the Institute's webpage, in the narrative, click on the words, "Choice Theory". Then click on the words "Reality Therapy".) The teacher and the student identify the misbehavior and why the behavior was inappropriate. It is helpful to try to determine what the student wanted when misbehaving. The student must accept responsibility for the behavior and work with the teacher to develop a plan.

> ### Questions for the Student[4]
>
> When you behaved as you did, what did you want?
> What did you do?
> Did what you did get you what you wanted?
> What could you do next time to get what you wanted?

When an acceptable plan has been developed, the student needs to commit to following the plan that has been agreed on. It is sometimes helpful to have the student sign the plan to indicate his or her agreement with the plan. This establishes a record of the plan.

If the student follows the plan agreed upon, the teacher provides positive feedback. If the student does not follow the terms of the plan, a new plan is made. This problem solving model can be help the student to accept responsibility for his or her behavior and to have ownership of a plan to correct the behavior.

Bullying

Bullying is a serious problem in today's schools. According to the Department of Justice, bullying is defined as 'repeated physical, verbal, or psychological attacks or intimidation directed against a victim who cannot properly defend himself or herself because of size or strength or because the victim is outnumbered or less psychologically resilient' than those doing the bullying. Some of the actions classified as bullying include: name calling, assault, intimidation, spreading rumors, making demands for money, theft of possessions, and destruction of property.[5]

Teachers can help reduce the problem of bullying by *actively supervising* their students in the classroom and on the playground. Letting students know that they are being observed and are accountable for their behavior can create a more safe environment for students.

A high level of *trust* between students and teacher will encourage students who observe bullying activities to report them to the teacher. Teaching students conflict management skills can also be useful in preventing and dealing with bullying.

The National Education Association's Bullying and Sexual Harassment Prevention and Intervention Program suggests that one of the most important ways to deal with bullying is to get students called *bystanders* involved. A bystander is a student who is not the victim of bullying and is not the bully. Bystanders are encouraged to step in and let the bully know their behavior is unacceptable and will not be tolerated.

To help students learn to intervene effectively when they see bullying taking place, teachers and other school personnel need to model the conversations students need to have and to encourage the students to intervene. According to the NEA, this approach is effective in school setting such as hallways and cafeterias and in online communities as well.[6]

At the school level, it is important to have bullying prevention programs in place that are developmentally appropriate for the different ages and abilities of students in the school. The school also needs to develop policies for dealing with bullying behavior when it does occur.

Bullying Resources
www.nea.org/bullying

Bullying Handout
www.kidsareworthit.com

Stop Bullying
http://stopbullyingnow.hrsa.gov/

"CBS: The Dangers of Bullying Interview of Barbara Coloroso"

"Bystanders Over Bullies – BOB"

Summary

The strategies the teacher uses to manage his or her classroom should be correlated with his or her beliefs about teaching and student learning. Students need a safe and orderly classroom environment in order to be academically and socially productive. In a safe and orderly environment, teachers can help students to learn to make good choices and to accept responsibility for their behavior.

Students are more likely to put forth effort to learn when their needs are met by the teacher and the teacher's strategies. When student needs are met and clear and consistent expectations are provided by the teacher, students can experience academic and social success in the classroom.

Positive reinforcement and feedback recognize appropriate behavior in the classroom. Teachers can use a variety of management strategies to deal appropriately with minor misbehavior, chronic misbehavior, and serious misbehavior. Students will be less likely to misbehave when they feel safe, when their needs are met, and when they are appropriately recognized for appropriate behavior.

Additional Resources

Burke, K. (2008). *What to Do with the Kid Who ...: Developing Cooperation, Self-Discipline, and Responsibility in the Classroom* (3rd ed.). Thousand Oaks, CA: Corwin.

Hunter, M. (1990). *Discipline That Develops Self-Discipline*. Thousand Oaks, CA: Corwin.

Kapalka, G. (2009). *Eight Steps to Classroom Management*. Thousand Oaks, CA: Corwin.

Kottler, J. A., & Kottler, E. (2009). *Students Who Drive You Crazy: Succeeding with Resistant, Unmotivated, and Otherwise Difficult Young People.*(2nd ed.). Thousand Oaks, CA: Corwin.

Payne, R. K. (2006). *Working with Students: Discipline Strategies for the Classroom.* Highlands, TX: aha! Process.

Reider, B. (2005). *Teach More and Discipline Less: Preventing Problem Behaviors in the K-6 Classroom.* Thousand Oaks, CA: Corwin.

Footnotes

[1] Weinstein, C. S., Romano, M. E., & Mignano, A. J., Jr. (2011). *Elementary Classroom Management: Lessons from Research and Practice.* New York, NY: McGraw-Hill.

[2] Hunter, M. (1987). *Discipline with Dignity.* Videotape. El Segundo, CA: Special Purpose Films.

[3] Coloroso, B. (1990). *Winning at Teaching without Beating Your Kids.* Littleton, CO: Kids Are Worth It. (DVD)

[4] Glasser, W., & Mentley, K. (1996). *Building a Quality School: A Matter of Responsibility.* Port Chester, NY: National Professional Resources. (Videotape)

[5] Retrieved December 30, 2010, from www.cops.usdoj.gov/files/RIC/Publications/e07063414-guide.pdf

[6] Flannery, M. E. (2011). Does It Get Better? *NEA Today, 29* (3), January/February, 2011, p. 38-40.

Chapter Four
Creating the Classroom Community
The Group Building Process

"Forks High School had a frightening total of only three hundred and fifty-seven – now – fifty-eight students; there were more than seven hundred people in my junior class alone back home. All of the kids here had grown up together – their grandparents had been toddlers together. I would be the new girl from the big city, a curiosity, a freak."

Bella Swan in *Twilight*
Stephenie Meyer, Little, Brown and Company, 2005

"Too many students in America go to school in a traditional, lonely classroom where they are isolated from their peers and are taught to learn in silence. …
Too often, spontaneity and student interaction are punished."

Larry Lyman & Harvey Foyle
*Cooperative Grouping for Interactive Learning:
Students, Teachers, and Administrators*
National Educational Association, 1990

Caring and Productive Classroom Communities

In previous chapters, strategies for creating the safe and orderly classroom – which is essential for learning to occur – were discussed. Increasing student diversity, demands for accountability, rapid societal change, and an expanding curriculum are some of the factors that have created a need for safe and orderly classrooms to also become caring and productive classroom communities in order to meet the many challenges facing students and teachers.

Caring and productive classroom communities are need fulfilling places where the psychological needs of students can be met. The classroom community helps to meet students' needs for acceptance by promoting friendship, empathy, and respect for diversity. Power is shared with students who have developmentally appropriate responsibilities for helping each other to learn, for taking care of the classroom, and for doing their personal best. Freedom allows students to make appropriate choices, to express themselves creatively, and to make mistakes. As students work together and become a more cohesive team, learning becomes fun and productivity increases.[1] Faith Moran wrote a poem about herself and how she views her own identity.

Communities are positive places in which teachers connect personally with each student and help the students make connections to what is being learned. Students are encouraged to connect with other students in the class and to feel a sense of belonging and pride in being a part of the community. The unique talents and perspectives of every student are recognized and celebrated. One of the many benefits of the classroom community is that interaction with others provides opportunities for each student to gain insight into his or her personal strengths and weaknesses.[2]

Caring and productive classroom communities model and implement the tenets of American democratic society. Classroom communities are democratic when all members are expected to share in the work, help to make decisions, and receive benefits. Teachers appropriately share the responsibilities for the successful functioning of the classroom with students, depending on their developmental levels. For example, students may be responsible for many of the routine activities needed to keep the class operating. Teachers are careful not to do anything for students that they could do for themselves.[3]

One teacher, Billie Manderick, wrote about building a classroom community and its impact on her students.

Group Building

As the economic resources available for schools decline in many places, teachers need to be sure to utilize the potential of positive student interaction in the classroom community as a resource for increasing student productivity and satisfaction. However, caring and productive classroom communities do not occur by chance. Group building activities are needed to provide awareness of and respect for others, to nurture student self-esteem, to facilitate communication, and to help students learn social skills. Group building activities are especially important at the beginning of the school year as the classroom community is being created. Throughout the school year, group building activities continue to sustain and enhance the caring and productive environment.

One important thing an effective teacher needs to do is to have something for the students to do when they walk in the door. This establishes your expectations for what they should do every morning when they enter your classroom. In addition, utilizing an activity that students can work independently ensures that class time is being used wisely and students understand that learning will begin as soon as they enter the classroom. The first day activity needs to be something that helps excite and motivate students about the new school year. The *Day of Firsts* group building activity is an example of an activity that can be used for this purpose. Activities that are used after the first day can be activities that build students' background about the topic of the day or review important prerequisite skills for that day's lesson.

When students enter the room ask them to find the preassigned seat and begin to work on the activity on their desk. Share with students that each morning they will come into the classroom and begin their morning work activity immediately. Make sure to stress that students need to work independently and do their very best. If there is an answer they are unsure of, it is okay to skip it or make an educated guess. After students have worked independently for a few minutes, have students work with their table partners to add or change in answers to their assignment. When the table groups have had the opportunity to discuss their answers, then go over the answers as a whole group. The activity was created so that students will be able to answer some questions independently, some they will be able to answer when they work with a small group of other students, and still others will only be able to be answered with the help of the teacher.

After going through all the answers, explain to students that this activity represents how the school year will go. This year there might be concepts or questions that you already know, such as some of the questions from this activity. If there is something that you already know, then it is your job to help others around you so that they can be successful as well. Students will have different strengths and everyone will need to work together to ensure everyone in our classroom community is successful. Likewise, there will be some concepts that we can only fully understand if we construct our knowledge with other students. Finally, there will be some concepts that we will only be able to master with the help of the educator. Overall, the only way that we can be completely successful is to work together and use everyone's strengths to grow and learn. This will help students to understand your educational philosophy as well as establish their role in the classroom community.

The group building process helps students experience the benefits of working together. Trust is built as students experience mutual regard and appreciation for the diversity of their peers. In the classroom community, students need to have many opportunities to communicate with each other in different ways. As classrooms become increasingly diverse, strategies for helping students communicate with others who speak a different language may be needed or who communicate in different ways, such as sign language.

Group building activities need to provide opportunities for all students to regularly experience success during the group building process. The theory of multiple intelligences suggests that each student has unique abilities that he or she brings to the classroom community. Group building activities that require different intelligences should be used. For example, a group member who was frustrated by a critical thinking group builder which required verbal intelligence may be able to be a leader in his or her group when a musical group builder taps an area of personal strength.

"Group Building Activity – Middle School Example"

Components of the Group Building Process[4]

1. Heterogeneous grouping – Students have the opportunity to work with other students in the class on a regular basis. During the first weeks of school, every student should have the opportunity to interact with every other student in some type of cooperative activity.

2. Positive interdependence – Group building tasks are structured so that students need to work together to be successful in completing the task.

3. Individual accountability – All students are held accountable by the teacher for active and positive participation and for doing their part in completing the task.

4. Group reward – Appropriate group building activities help to meet students' needs for acceptance, power, freedom, and fun. Group products can be displayed in the classroom.

5. Success – Group building activities need to be designed so that students can be successful in working together. Group grading of group building activities will often discourage cooperative efforts.

Using Multiple Intelligences in the Group Building Process

In the following overview of multiple intelligences theory, suggestions for incorporating each of the intelligence areas as part of a productive classroom are provided. In addition, group building activities for each of the intelligence areas are provided. An activity for younger students and one for older students will be provided for each area. These group building activities are designed to appeal to a wide range of learners and can be adapted for the interests and abilities of the teacher's own class. For most of the group building activities, the group reward is that the activity is fun for the students.

Teachers' editions of student textbooks, teacher magazines, popular media, and many websites offer additional ideas for group building activities linked to specific content areas and standards. Some resources are provided at the end of this chapter.

When using other materials, teachers should always observe *copyright laws and regulations*. Copyright information can be found at Stanford University. A copyright tutorial is located at Brigham Young University.

Copyright Information (Stanford University)
http://fairuse.stanford.edu/Copyright_and_Fair_Use_Overview/

Copyright Tutorial (Brigham Young University)
http://www.lib.byu.edu/departs/copyright/tutorial/intro/page1.htm

Multiple Intelligences

Students bring a variety of intelligences to the elementary or middle school classroom. According to Howard Gardner, Harvard University, every human being possesses a unique combination of these eight intelligences.

> Verbal intelligence
>
> Logical and mathematical intelligence
>
> Visual intelligence
>
> Music intelligence
>
> Body intelligence
>
> People intelligence
>
> Self intelligence
>
> Nature intelligence

"Howard Gardner Explains His Multiple Intelligence Theory in this Edutopia Video Clip"

"Howard Gardner Explains His Theory When Interviewed on ANA in the Philippines"

Traditional teaching and testing have relied too heavily on verbal and logical and mathematical intelligences. As a result, too many students have not been as successful in school as they could be. To help these students, the question we need to be asking, according to Gardner, is not "is the student smart?" but rather, "how is the student smart?"[5] A fun quiz based upon Howard Gardner's multiple intelligences can be an entertaining way for students to determine their intelligences.

Teachers can use the multiple intelligences to accommodate the learning needs of their students. By varying instructional strategies to accommodate different intelligence strengths, the teachers can help more students to be successful.[6] Children's needs change from the time they are babies to the time they are in school. Teachers work with the children's potential, not knowing how their intelligences will be transformed from babies to school children to adults.

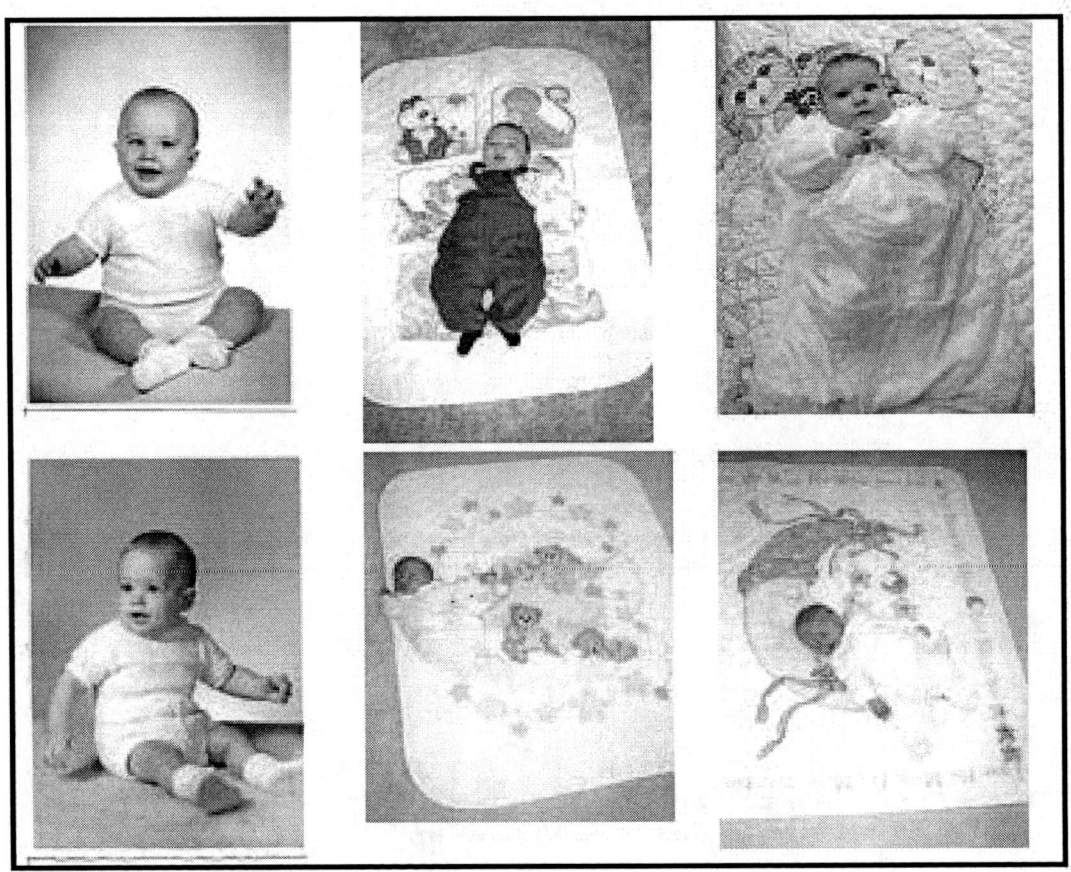

Verbal Intelligence

Students who are strong in the area of verbal intelligence usually read, write, and speak well. Because they express themselves well in words, they are usually successful in most classroom settings. To help all students achieve this success, the teacher must create a literate classroom environment that encourages all students to read, write, and communicate orally with others.

Suggestions for Encouraging Verbal Intelligence

1. Provide time for reading and writing activities that promote involvement and success for all students.

2. Encourage students to express themselves orally in individual student conferences with the teacher, in collaborative and cooperative groups, and in class meetings.

3. Have a variety of books, magazines, and other reading material available in the classroom. Riddles and jokes appeal to many students. At the *Yahoo! Kids* webpage, there are over 2110 jokes provided.

4. When giving oral directions, have one or more students repeat the directions for the class before students begin work. Students can be overwhelmed by directions given by the teacher.

5. Provide daily time for independent reading and for the teacher to read to the class.

Younger Students Group Building Activity for Verbal Intelligence	Getting to Know You
Older Students Group Building Activity for Verbal Intelligence	Matching Game

Logical and Mathematical Intelligence

Many students become discouraged because they find problem solving and math difficult. Students need to have regular practice in solving problems that require both critical and creative thinking. For younger students, concrete examples and the use of manipulatives can help students to understand. Making problem solving seem like play will encourage student involvement and interest.

Suggestions for Encouraging Logical and Mathematical Intelligence

1. Have a problem of the day for students to solve that involves critical or creative thinking. Vary the difficulty of the problem so all students can be successful at times.

2. Help students learn basic math facts to build confidence and accuracy in math.

3. When students are solving problems, encourage students to share strategies they use to solve problems so that students learn that many strategies for solving problems are available.

4. Have students make up problems and questions.

5. Ask higher level questions which require students to apply, analyze, synthesize, and evaluate what they are learning.

Younger Students Group Building Activity for Logical and Mathematical Intelligence	Feed the Turkey
Older Students Group Building Activity for Logical and Mathematical Intelligence	By the Numbers

Visual Intelligence

Pictures, diagrams, charts, and graphic organizers can provide a great deal of information for students. Visual representations of information and ideas can help students who may be having difficulty with reading comprehension. Encourage students to read and discuss the graphics that accompany the written text in books, as these graphics often contain valuable information and clues to the content of the written text.

Suggestions for Encouraging Visual Intelligence

1. Use pictures, posters, DVD's, and online visual resources.

2. Use graphic organizers to help students understand and organize information.

3. Be alert to the visual content of books and web resources. Are all students represented?

4. Take snapshots of students regularly and display them.

5. Give students a bulletin board area to display items that are important to them.

Younger Students Group Building Activity for Visual Intelligence	Class-a-Pede
Older Students Group Building Activity for Visual Intelligence	Class Quilt

Music Intelligence

Music and rhythm come easily to some students. Introducing music into lessons can promote involvement and interest for students. Even though a music class is usually offered for most elementary school students, music and rhythm activities can be productively used in the regular classroom as well.

Suggestions for Encouraging Music Intelligence

1. Use background music to accompany some transition and study periods.

2. Use music to relax students when they come back into the classroom after recess or physical education.

3. Consult with the music teacher for ideas to enhance what you are teaching.

4. Use poetry, chants, and choral reading.

5. Try a rhythmic clapping pattern or a rain stick to engage the students' attention.

Younger Students Group Building Activity for Music Intelligence	Sing-a-Song
Older Students Group Building Activity for Music Intelligence	That's All Folks!

Body Intelligence

The ability to move gracefully and to control fine and gross motor movement is what makes athletes, dancers, and surgeons excel. Many students with strong body intelligence find it difficult to sit still as long as they are required to in the classroom and become frustrated when they are asked to work without moving around. There are difference between competitive and cooperative games. Several cooperative body games are available and described by Bill Stinson.

Suggestions for Encouraging Body Intelligence

1. Try a warm-up period of light exercise at the beginning of the day to help students become awake and alert.

2. Stop periodically to take a stretch break.

3. Use activities like "Simon Says" to practice verbal and body skills.

4. Teach students non-competitive games that require cooperation.

5. Emphasize the importance of regular exercise for all students.

Younger Students Group Building Activity Body Intelligence	We're Connected!
Older Students Group Building Activity Body Intelligence	What I Did Last Summer

"Visual and body Intelligence in Third/Fourth Grade Health Activity"

People Intelligence

Getting along with others is a skill that will be required of all students in order to be successful in life. Students can learn to get along with others, especially those different from themselves, when regular opportunities for collaboration and cooperation are provided in the classroom. Reducing or eliminating competition in the classroom can help students to get along more successfully. Of course, all group building activities require interpersonal intelligence as well as other primary intelligences.

Suggestions for Encouraging People Intelligence

1. Use group building activities like the ones suggested in this chapter to nurture a classroom community at the beginning of the school year.

2. Involve students in collaborative and cooperative activities as part of the instructional program.

3. Teach social and communication skills.

4. Hold regular classroom meetings to encourage group communication and problem solving.

5. Teach conflict management and peer mediation skills as developmentally appropriate.

Younger Students Group Building Activity for People Intelligence	Just Like Me!
Older Students Group Building Activity for People Intelligence	Alike and Different

"Fifth Grade Group Building – Dynamic Duo Activity"

Self Intelligence

All students need to develop self-awareness, esteem, and confidence. When students know their individual strengths and capabilities, they have the power to be successful and to take responsibility for their successes and mistakes. William Glasser's Choice Theory, discussed in another chapter, can be integrated into the structure of the classroom to encourage responsibility for behavior and for decisions that the students make.

"William Glasser Tells about Reality Therapy and Choice Theory"

Suggestions for Encouraging Self Intelligence

1. Encourage students to write written reflections in journals.

2. Teach Choice Theory to students as developmentally appropriate.

3. Encourage self-evaluation.

4. Help students build portfolios of their work to share with peers and family members.

5. Help each child to identify areas of personal strength.

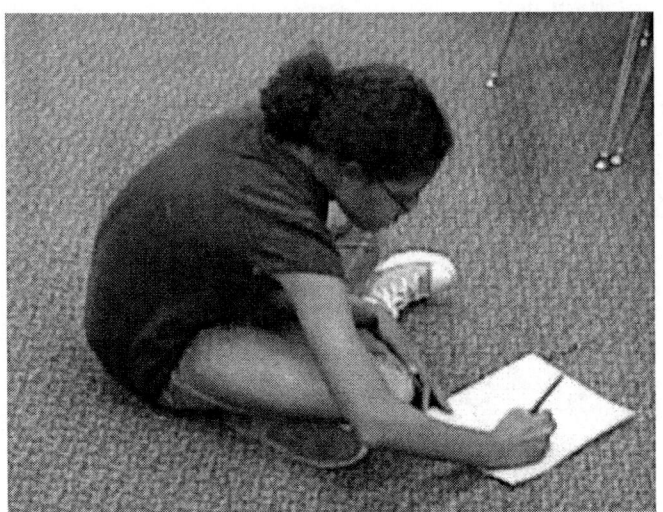

Younger Students Group Building Activity for Self Intelligence	Show and Share
Older Students Group Building Activity for Self Intelligence	Sharing Teams

Nature Intelligence

Knowledge about the environment and skill in identifying characteristics of animals and plants are strengths of the student with natural intelligence. By making the classroom an extension of the outdoors as appropriate, students with this intelligence strength will feel more comfortable. Nature becomes part of the learning environment.

"'When Learning Comes Naturally' Shows Students Learning from Nature"

Suggestions for Encouraging Nature Intelligence

1. Have pictures and posters of nature in the classroom.

2. Bring plants into the classroom and have the students help to take care of them.

3. Bring pets into the classroom and have the students help to take care of them.

4. Take students outside and encourage them to observe.

Younger Students Group Building Activity for Nature Intelligence	Nature Walk
Older Students Group Building Activity for Nature Intelligence	Classifying Baseball Mascots

Observing Student Interaction During Group Building Activities

One of the benefits of group building activities for the teacher is the opportunity to get to know the students and observe them interacting with each other. Observing the students during group building activities helps the teacher analyze the academic and social skill levels of the students, to identify needed social and communication skills to teach, and to plan for appropriate group placements for future collaborative and cooperative activities. As the teacher observes the groups interacting, look for the following:

1. Which students are leaders in their groups?

2. Which students have good verbal skills?

3. Which students seem to be knowledgeable about the content they are working on?

4. Which students have good social skills?

5. Which students are shy or reticent in their groups?

6. Which students seem to need extra assistance or support to succeed in the group activity?

7. Which students seem to have trouble getting along with others in their groups?

8. What are some of the multiple intelligences strengths of individual students?

9. Overall, what cooperative skill(s) do groups seem to be demonstrating successfully as they work together? (to positively reinforce after the activity)

10. Overall, what cooperative skill(s) do groups seem to need more help with? (to teach them later)

Using Observational Data

1. Do group members understand why they are working together cooperatively? If not, how will you clarify the goals and benefits of working together in future collaborative and cooperative activities?

2. Are group members participating actively and positively in group building activities? If not, how will you encourage active, positive participation in future collaborative and cooperative activities? If participation was active and positive, be sure to give the students positive feedback.

3. What skills do the group members lack to work together collaboratively and cooperatively? How will you teach these skills?

4. Was the noise level appropriate during the group work? If not, practice the signal for stopping and review the expectations. If the students did well, be sure to give them positive feedback.

5. If movement was necessary during the task, was it accomplished safely and with a minimum of distraction? If problems occurred, what will you do to prevent problems in future collaborative and cooperative activities? If the students did well, be sure to give them positive feedback.

Involving Family Members in the Group Building Process

Group building activities can be structured so that some of the answers to a particular activity may not be generated by the students. Students can be encouraged to go home and check with family members to see if they can assist with any of the answers the class has not thought of during school time. Family members can also be encouraged to come up with other examples for the activity. (Additional suggestions for involving family members can be found in another chapter.) Food Fantasy is an example of a group building activity that could involve assistance from family members.

Summary

Caring and productive classroom communities do not occur by chance. The benefits of mutual respect, self-esteem, friendship, and responsibility that come from participating in a classroom community require a commitment of time and energy to the process of group building and identifying the strengths of each student in the class. Teachers who build caring and productive classroom communities realize that student interaction in the classroom is powerful learning tool that can improve achievement, encourage positive student attitudes, and enhance the student's desire to learn.[7]

Selected Children's Books
About Working Together and Getting Along

Cooper, M., & Gottlieb, D. (1995). *I Got Community*. New York, NY: Henry Holt.
Creech, S., & Bliss, H. (2001). *A Fine, Fine School*. New York, NY: Scholastic.
Lester, H., & Munsinger, H. (1988). *Tacky the Penguin*. New York, NY: Houghton Mifflin.
Lionni, L. (1967). *Frederick*. New York, NY: Alfred P. Knopf.
Lobel, A. (1970). *Frog and Toad Are Friends*. New York, NY: HarperCollins.
Naylor, P. R., & Ramsey, M. (2005). *Anyone Can Eat Squid!* Tarrytown, NY: Marshall Cavendish.
Raschka, C. (1993). *Yo! Yes?* New York, NY: Scholastic.
Rohmann, E. (2002). *My Friend Rabbit*. New York, NY: Macmillan.
Steptoe, J., & Lewis, E. B. (1997). *Creativity*. New York, NY: Clarion Books.
Thaler, M., & Lee, J. (2004). *The New Kid from the Black Lagoon*. New York, NY: Scholastic.

Additional Resources

Armstrong, T. (2009). *Multiple Intelligences in the Classroom* (3rd ed.). Alexandria, VA: Association for Supervision and Curriculum Development.

"Thomas Armstrong Discusses His Book and the Multiple Intelligences Theory"

Armstrong, T. (2002). *You're Smarter Than You Think: A Kid's Guide to Multiple Intelligences.* Minneapolis, MN: Free Spirit.

Csikszentmihalyi, M. (2008). *Flow: The Psychology of Optimal Experience (P. S.).* New York, NY: Harper Perennial.

Foyle, H. C., Lyman, L., & Thies, S. A. (1991). Group Building for Cooperation. *Cooperative Learning in the Early Childhood Classroom.* Washington, DC: National Education Association.

Gardner, H. (1983). *Frames of Mind: The Theory of Multiple Intelligences.* New York, NY: Basic Books.

Gardner, H. (2006). *Multiple Intelligences: New Horizons in Theory and Practice.* New York, NY: Basic Books.

Goleman, D. (1995). *Emotional Intelligence: Why It Can Mean More Than IQ.* New York, NY: Bantam.

Goleman, D. (2006). *Social Intelligence: The New Science of Human Relationships.* New York, NY: Bantam Dell.

Kagan, L., Kagan, M., & Kagan, S. (1997). *Cooperative Learning Structures for Teambuilding.* San Clemente, CA: Kagan Cooperative Learning.

Luvmor, J., & Luvmor S. (2007). *Everyone Wins! Cooperative Games and Activities.* Garbiola Island, British Columbia: New Society Publishers.

Lyman, L., Foyle, H. C., & Azwell, T. S. (1993). Restructuring the Classroom for Cooperation. *Cooperative Learning in the Elementary Classroom.* Washington, DC: National Education Association.

MacGregor, M. G. (2007). *Teambuilding with Teens: Activities for Leadership, Decision Making, and Group Success.* Minneapolis, MN: Free Spirit.

Smith, M. K. (2008, 2002). Howard Gardner and multiple intelligences. *the encyclopedia of informal education,* http://www.infed.org/thinkers/gardner.htm.

Stinson, W., Mehrhof, J. H., & Thies, S. A. (1993). *Quality Thematic Lesson Plans for Classroom Teachers: Movement Activities for Pre-K and Kindergarten.* Kendall/Hunt.

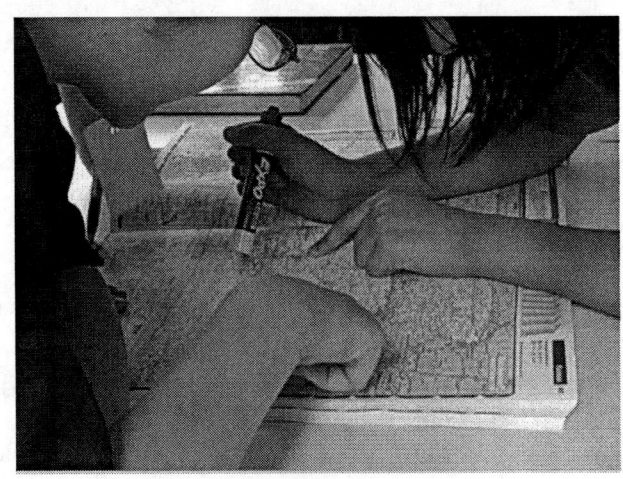

Footnotes

[1] Lyman, L., & Foyle, H. C. (1990). *Cooperative Grouping for Interactive Learning: Students, Teachers, and Administrators.* Washington, DC: National Education Association, p. 9-22.

[2] Lyman, L., & Foyle, H. C. (1998). Facilitating Collaboration in Schools. *Teaching and Change. 5*, 3-4, Spring-Summer, 1998, p. 312-339.

[3] Azwell, T. S., Foyle, H. C., Lyman, L., & Smith, N. L (1999). *Constructing Curriculum in Context.* Dubuque, IA: Kendall/Hunt, p. 403-404.

[4] Lyman, L., Foyle, H. C., & Azwell, T. S. (1993). *Cooperative Learning in the Elementary Classroom.* Washington, DC: National Education Association, p. 19-27.

[5] ABC News. (1993). *Common Miracles: The New American Revolution in Learning.* New York, NY: MPI Video.

[6] Gardner, H. (1995). Multiple Intelligences. *Early Childhood Today*, August/September, 1995, p. 29-31.

[7] Lyman & Foyle. (1990). pages 64 and 65.

Chapter Five
Maintaining and Enhancing the Classroom Community

"Gloria is in the second grade, too. Gloria is big.
She is bigger than I am. We became friends because we are big,
but we stay friends because we like each other."

Big Bob and the Thanksgiving Potatoes
Daniel and Jill Pinkwater, Scholastic, 1998

Classroom communities can be built with some effort on the part of teacher and students. To function effectively as members of a community, students need to have clear and consistent rules and procedures and have opportunities to practice these expectations. Group building activities help students get acquainted and develop friendships with other students in the classroom.

The classroom community requires regular nurturing in order to maintain and enhance the positive classroom environment and positive student interactions that are taking place during the group building process. The classroom community can be enhanced by incorporating rituals, traditions, and appropriate celebrations into the culture of the classroom. Opportunities for students to interact and continue to learn more about each other also provides opportunities to nurture the classroom community.

In every group where people work together, conflict is inevitable. Helping children learn and practice skills for managing conflict can help to maintain mutual respect and friendship in the classroom. Working together on class projects to help others is also an effective way to enhance the classroom community.

Encouraging Interest and Involvement with Class Ritualsand Traditions

Making *rituals and traditions* a part of the classroom culture encourages student interest and involvement while building and nurturing the classroom community. Rituals and traditions will differ depending on the personality of the teacher and the age and developmental levels of the students.

Some Possible Rituals and Traditions for the Classroom

1. time for sharing each day

2. daily quote or poem with an inspirational message
   www.heartsandminds.org/quotes/quotes.htm

3. daily cartoon, joke, or riddle
   www.internet4classrooms.com/daily_dose.htm
   www.scatty.com

4. classroom theme, mascot, nickname chosen by the students
   http://en.wikipedia.org/wiki/List_of_college_mascots_in_the_United_States`

5. share classroom jobs and responsibilities

6. service projects in the school or community
   http://www.nylc.org/

7. class motto, cheer, song, or poem

8. newsletter to family members authored by the students
   http://k6educators.about.com/od/classroommanagement/a/weeklynews.htm

9. class web site

10. student star of the week
    http://www.sanchezclass.com/starstudent.htm

Some Special Days to Celebrate

Halloween and Valentine's Day traditionally provided two of the very limited opportunities for students to *celebrate* together. By structuring academic skills around special days and weeks more frequently, the teacher can generate excitement and interest in the curriculum.

School Starts	First day of school www.proteacher.com/030005.shtml www.icebreakers.ws/ www2.scholastic.com/browse/article.jsp?id=3340
September 13, 1857	Milton Hershey's birthday www.hersheys.com
September 17, 1787	United States Constitution Day www.archives.gov/education/lessons/constitution-day/
September 24, 1936	Jim Henson, creator of the Muppets, born www.muppetcentral.com
October 2, 1950	'Peanuts' comic strip first appeared in newspapers http.comics.com/peanuts
October 14, 1890	Dwight D. Eisenhower born www.eisenhower.archives.gov
October 27, 1858	Theodore Roosevelt born www.theodoreroosevelt.org/kidscorner/tr_teddy.htm
November 8, 1836	Milton Bradley born www.ehow.com/facts_4925703_history-milton-bradley-games.html

November 29	1832	Louisa May Alcott born www.louisamayalcott.org
	1898	C. S. Lewis born www.harpercollinschildrens.com/kids/gamesandcontests/features/princecaspian
	1918	Madeleine L'Engle born www.bookrags.com/A_Wrinkle_in_Time
December 1, 1955		Rosa Parks refuses to give up her seat on a bus www.achievement.org/autodoc/page/par0bio-1
December 5, 1901		Walt Disney born www.disney.go.com
January 15, 1929		Martin Luther King, Jr. born www.thekingcenter.org
January 22, 1907		Douglas "Wrong Way" Corrigan born www.centennialofflight.gov/essay/Explorers_Record_Setters_and_Daredevils/corrigan/EX16.htm
February 11, 1847		Thomas Edison born www.nps.gov/edis/forkids/index.htm
February 12, 1809		Abraham Lincoln born http://showcase.netins.net/web/creative/lincoln/education/failures.htm
March 2, 1904		Dr. Seuss born www.seussville.com
March 3, 1847		Alexander Graham Bell born www.crayola.com/lesson-plans/detail/can-you-hear-me?-lesson-plan/
April 5, 1761		Sibyl Ludington born www.nwhm.org/education-resources/biography/biographies/sibyl-ludington/
April 22, 1970		First Earth Day http://edhelper.com/caring_for_earth.htm

May 7   1833   Johannes Brahams born
                   www.dsokids.com/listen/ComposerDetail.aspx?composerID=18

                   1840   Peter Tchaikovsky born
                   www.dsokids.com/listen/composerdetail.aspx?composerid=35

May 15, 1856   L. Frank Baum born
                   www.thewizardofoz.info/ozteach.html

**For a daily overview of important happenings
on each day of the year,
go to this website:
www.history.com/this-day-in-history**

Examples of Activities for Students to Continue Forming Friendships

Group building activities help students to get acquainted and begin to form friendships. Too often, these activities are limited to the first weeks of school. In order to maintain the classroom community, students need regular chances to interact with each other and continue the process of building and nurturing friendships. Some suggested activities follow.

Stick to Saying Good Things

Sheila Broyles

A different kindergarten student is selected each day to be the 'Stick to Saying Good Things' student. The students say good things about the student as the teacher records the ideas on masking tape or sticky notes. The tape or sticky notes are placed on the student.

Surprise Bag

Sheila Broyles

Students take turns choosing an item with their family members at home to put in the surprise bag. The student and family members write down three clues to the object on a piece of paper and send the clues and the object to school in the surprise bag.

Example: It is little.
You use it with your hands.
It makes holes.

What is it? (a paper punch)

Class Poem

Students are grouped in heterogeneous groups of 3 or 4. The teacher shows the class the format which will be used to create a class poem. Each group is then asked to think of several ideas for each stanza in case groups come up with the same idea. The teacher asks the groups to share answers that are recorded on the smart board or on a sheet of chart paper. The class works together to edit the poem by rearranging ideas for clarity and symmetry. The final version of the poem can be displayed in the classroom or shared with family members in the class newsletter.

We are a thoughtful and caring class.

We are happy when … (one line from each group)

We are a thoughtful and caring class.

We wish … (one line from each group)

We are a thoughtful and caring class.

We are worried about … (one line from each group)

We are a thoughtful and caring class.

We are trying hard to … (one line from each group)

Extending the activity – Other poetry writing ideas can be found at the following websites:

Writing Poems with Kids
www.suite101.com/content/writing-poems-with-kids-a23148

Jack Prelutsky
http://teacher.scholastic.com/writewit/poetry/jack_home.htm

Classroom Poll

The teacher groups the students in eight heterogeneous groups. Each student gets a copy of the question sheet and marks the answer he or she chooses for each item. Students cut out their answers. The teacher assigns each group one of the topics to tally (for example, ice cream flavors) and a collector for each group collects the responses for their topic from each student. Each group tallies the responses and constructs a graph of their data to share with the class. Completed graphs are posted on a bulletin board.

How many brothers and sisters do you have? 0 1 2 3 4 or more	What is your favorite color? Blue Red Yellow Green Another color
In what season is your birthday? Spring Summer Fall Winter	What is your favorite flavor of ice cream? Vanilla Chocolate Strawberry Chocolate Chip Another flavor
What is your favorite subject in school? Reading Social Studies Math Science Another subject	What is your favorite pet? Dog Cat Fish Bird Another pet
What is your favorite holiday? Halloween Thanksgiving Christmas Fourth of July Another holiday	What color are your eyes? Blue Brown Green Another color Don't know

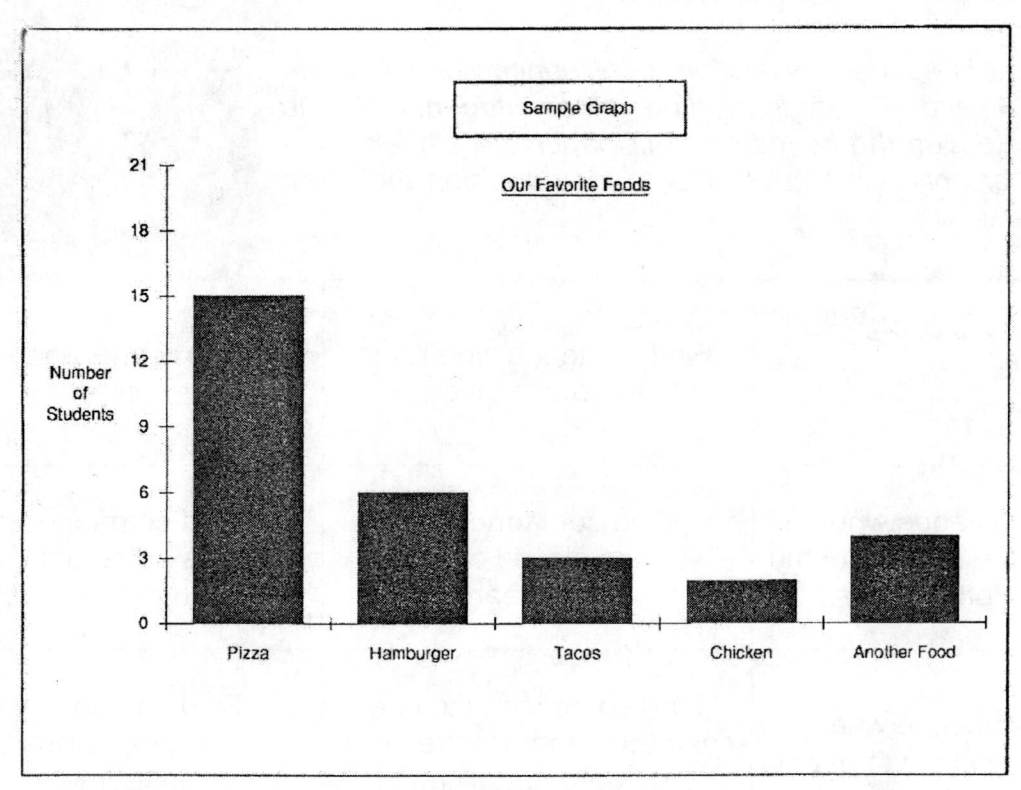

People Search

This activity is based the multiple intelligences described in chapters 4 and 5. Students find other students in the classroom to sign the boxes on their papers. A student may sign a paper only one time. Students may not sign their own paper.

Find someone who likes to draw or doodle.	Find someone who likes to go camping.	Find someone who likes to sing.
Find someone who has read one or more of the Harry Potter books.	Find someone who has played on a sports team.	Find someone who needs some quiet time alone now and then.
Find someone who can tell you the street address of the school.	Find someone who has had their name written on the board for talking in class.	Find someone who can play a musical instrument.
Find someone who keeps a journal or diary.	Find someone who knows the zip code of the place where we live.	Find someone who watched television before they came to school today.
Find someone who doesn't like to sit still.	Find someone who has one or more pets at home.	Find someone who gets along well with other people.

Extending the activity – Another example can be found at the following web site:

**Scavenger activity
http://hubpages.com/hub/People-Scavenger-Hunt**

Working with Students to Manage Conflict in the Classroom

Conflict is common to every situation in which groups of people are working together. When conflict is not occurring, it often means that that conflict is present but is not being acknowledged or dealt with effectively. Since students will experience conflict with others throughout their lives, it is important to help students acquire the skills needed to manage conflicts with others constructively.

Common ways of dealing with conflict include *denial*, *confrontation*, and *problem solving*. *Denying* that conflict is taking place is unproductive and may encourage bullying. While it may sometimes be necessary for the teacher to *confront* students who are involved in conflicts with each other, allowing the students to confront each other can cause conflicts to escalate. *Problem solving* strategies can help students work out solutions to conflicts in positive and productive ways.

Communication skills, especially active listening skills, are essential to managing conflict successfully by problem solving. When conflict is acknowledged and dealt with in positive and effective ways, classrooms are safer, happier, and more productive places to be.

Classroom Conflict
www.ideamarketers.com/?classroom_conflict_resolution&articleid=1255138

Cliques in the Classroom
http://www2.scholastic.com/browse/article.jsp?id=2120

Conflict can be caused by a number of different situations. Common *causes* for conflict (with examples that will help students understand) include:

1. Conflicts about sharing limited resources
   a. Family members with one television disagree about which show to watch.
   b. A student is accused by his classmates of "hogging" the drinking fountain.

2. Conflicts about wanting someone's attention
   a. Two students want their teacher's help at the same time.
   b. A girl wants a classmate to be her "only" best friend.

3. Conflicts because of different points of view
   a. Students can't agree about which student started the argument.
   b. Friends can't decide whom to support in the student election.

4. Conflicts caused by perceived unfairness or unkindness
   a. Students think their teacher plays favorites.
   b. A student is upset about the "mean thing" his friend said to him.

5. Conflicts arising from different personalities or customs
   a. Students are reluctant to include a new girl in their group – "she's not our kind".
   b. Students make fun of a classmate who has a different regional accent.

6. Conflicts about right or wrong and safety
   a. A girl encourages a friend to lie to her mother.
   b. A boy tells his friend to help him put graffiti on the bathroom wall.

There are several possible *outcomes* of conflict. The goal is for everyone in the conflict to believe that they have 'won' – that is, that a fair and equitable solution to the conflict has been found or that the parties in the conflict have agreed to disagree and move on.

Possible Outcomes of Conflict

win-win (everyone is happy with the solution)
win-lose (one student or group is happy, one is unhappy)
lose-win (the other student or group is happy, the other one is unhappy)
lose-lose (everyone is unhappy)
agree to disagree (everyone agrees to move on)

When conflicts do occur, teachers need to consider the developmental levels of the students when deciding how to involve the students in appropriate *problem solving* activities. A useful process for problem solving would include the following steps. It is essential that what the teacher decides is appropriate for the students.

Problem Solving Process

1. Identify the problem to be solved

2. Identify who is affected by the problem

3. Decide on how the conflict could be managed

4. Brainstorm ideas and solutions

5. Determine which ideas are the best

6. Agree on an idea to try

7. If the idea works, celebrate; if not, try one of the other ideas that was brainstormed

8. If a workable solution cannot be found in the time available, agree to disagree (move on)

Older students may be taught peer mediation skills to help fellow students solve disputes. Peer mediation can be used with students of the same age or with older students helping younger children. When used appropriately, peer mediation can reduce the amount of time teachers spend trying to solve minor conflicts and empower students to become more responsible and caring.

CRE Connection Resources
www.creducation.org/cre/teachers

"James S. Wells, MD – Keeping Cool Under Pressure"

Examples of Activities for Practicing Conflict Management Skills

Famous Conflicts[1]

In heterogeneous groups, students name the person, character, or group who did not get along with the people below.

_____ 1. The Three Little Pigs
_____ 2. Snoopy (the World War I Flying Ace)
_____ 3. Bart Simpson
_____ 4. Elmer Fudd
_____ 5. Harry Potter
_____ 6. The Sheriff of Nottingham
_____ 7. Edward Cullen
_____ 8. Al Capone
_____ 9. Captain Ahab
_____ 10. The Hatfields
_____ 11. Katniss Everdeen
_____ 12. Popeye

Can your group think of other examples?

Answers to Famous Conflicts Activity

(Other answers may be possible)

Three Little Pigs and the Big Bad Wolf
Bart Simpson and Homer Simpson
Harry Potter and Voldemort
Edward Cullen and Jacob Black
Captain Ahab and Moby Dick
Katniss Everdeen and President Snow

Snoopy and the Red Baron
Elmer Fudd and Bugs Bunny
The Sheriff of Nottingham and Robin Hood
Al Capone and Elliot Ness
The Hatfields and the McCoys
Popeye and Bluto

Identifying Sources of Conflict[2]

Working in heterogeneous groups, students label the conflict situations with the correct source of the conflict.

limited resources   point of view
wanting someone's attention   unfairness or unkindness
different personalities or customs right or wrong/student safety

_____ 1. Students disagree about whether the runner was safe or not.
_____ 2. A boy wants to play with his friend's father's gun – "it isn't loaded, is it?"
_____ 3. Two siblings each want the last piece of cake at dinner.
_____ 4. Students tell jokes about someone from another country who is offended.
_____ 5. Students all want to sit beside the student teacher on the bus to the field trip.
_____ 6. A teenager wants to drive when he has had too much to drink.
_____ 7. The class is angry because the teacher promised them extra recess and changed her mind.
_____ 8. A group tells a new club member he or she must shoplift and item to be in the club.
_____ 9. Students don't want a 'nerd' to be in their group when they are working in class.
_____ 10. A kindergartener cries because he is the only student not invited to a party.

Activity Answers

1. different points of view
2. right or wrong/student safety
3. limited resources
4. unfairness or unkindness
5. wanting someone's attention
6. right or wrong/student safety
7. unfairness or unkindness
8. right or wrong/student safety
9. different personalities or customs (also unfairness or unkindness)
10. unkindness or unfairness

Identifying Feelings and Emotions

EMOTICONS

Emoticons are made by typing symbols from a keyboard. Usually they indicate a person's feelings about something. These symbols have been showing up on electronic bulletin boards. Figure out the meaning of each emoticon. Design new emoticons.

1. :-O
2. :*
3. ;)
4. :'(
5. :D
6. >:-<
7. %-(
8. :X
9. :)
10. :Q
11. :(
12. :P

Emoticons Answers

1. YELL
2. A KISS
3. WINK
4. CRY
5. LAUGHTER
6. ANGER
7. CONFUSION
8. MY LIPS ARE SEALED
9. SMILE
10. SMOKING
11. FROWN
12. STICK OUT TONGUE

Seeing the Other Side

The ability to understand and respect another point of view is an essential skill for dealing with others and managing conflicts.

1. Argue the Other Side

In heterogeneous groups, students think of reasons why familiar sayings are correct. The groups then think of reasons why the saying would *not* be correct.

Each group is assigned a saying and they share their ideas with the class when asked to do so.

   a. Two heads are better than one.
   b. It is better to give than to receive.
   c. The more, the merrier
   d. Too many cooks spoil the soup.
   e. A bird in the hand is worth two in the bush.
   f. Children should be seen and not heard.

2. Defend a different point of view[3]

Each heterogeneous group is assigned one of the examples. The groups share their ideas with the class when asked to do so.

> The teacher may want to share a book as an *activity starter*:
>
> *The True Story of the 3 Little Pigs,* J. Scieska and L. Smith, Puffin, 2006
>
> *The Three Little Wolves and the Big Bad Pig*, E. Trivizas and H. Oxenbury, McElderry, 1997

    a. Defend the wolf in the fairy tale "Little Red Riding Hood".
    b. Defend the trolls in the fairy tale "The Three Billy Goats Gruff".
    c. Defend the giant in the fairy tale "Jack and the Beanstalk".
    d. Defend the witch in the fairy tale "Snow White".
    e. Defend the stepsisters in the fairy tale "Cinderella".
    f. Defend the witch in the fairy tale "Hansel and Gretel".

3. State another student's point of view.

During class discussions and in conflict situations, it is sometimes helpful to ask students to accurately state how the other person or group feels and why they feel that way. The other person or group must agree that their point of view is accurately reflected. Students can often be more open to the ideas of others when this strategy is used.

4. Empathy

Promoting empathy for peers is an important part of conflict management. Ask students to describe the feelings of literary characters, historical figures, or their own classmates. The following questions may be helpful for small group or whole class discussions.

    a. How do you think _____ feels (felt)?
    b. How do you think you would feel if that happened to you?
    c. Has anything like that ever happened to you?
    d. What should _____ do if this happens again?
    e. Do you think it was easy for _____ to do what he or she did?
    f. What would you have done if you were in the same position?
    g. How could his or her friends help?

Tone of Voice

The *tone of voice* a speaker uses can provide information about the speaker's feelings, meaning, and point of view. The tone of voice can alter the meaning of the statement or idea. Students are placed in heterogeneous groups. Each group is given a list of statements and suggested feelings. Group members take turns using one of the statements and say it using a tone of voice which expresses one of the suggested feelings. Other group members try to guess the feeling being conveyed.

Statements	Feelings to Use		
"Oh, mother."	Surprise	boredom	fright
"That's interesting."	Happiness	sarcasm	disbelief
"I'm sure."	Sadness	admiration	pain
"Thanks a lot."	Jealousy	anger	others?
"Okay."			

Point of View

Understanding that others may have different *points of view* about things is an essential skill for managing conflicts. Students need to learn that different points of view do not represent a personal attack on their own views.

In heterogeneous groups, students identify the point of view on a given issue. Each student is assigned one of the points of view to represent.

Issue: School starts tomorrow. **Points of view:** a) a very successful student b) a student who struggles in class c) a parent tired of having the kids at home d) a teacher teaching for the first time	**Issue:** The school is considering requiring students to wear a uniform. **Points of view:** a) a student whose family is poor b) a student who loves trendy clothes c) a parent concerned about clothing fads d) a teacher tired of students making fun of what others are wearing

Anticipating Conflict

One of the most effective strategies for managing conflict is for the teacher to be able to recognize how conflict could occur in an activity, program, or situation and *proactively* plan strategies for minimizing the conflict that might occur. The following questions may be useful to teachers as they are planning instructional activities for students. For example, if a play the teacher is considering for the students to perform has a limited number of parts, the teacher would want to consider ways to make sure all students can be actively involved.

Planning to Deal with Potential Conflicts

1. What are possible sources of conflict, misunderstanding, or hurt feelings in this activity?

2. What groups or individual students may come into conflict during this activity?

3. What possible points of view or ideas could be expressed during this activity that could provoke conflict, misunderstanding, or hurt feelings?

4. How will resources (students, materials, time, teacher help) be allocated during this activity?

5. Will the scarcity of any needed resources (such as materials, computers, time, teacher help) cause conflict among students?

6. How can possible conflicts that may arise be prevented, minimized, or dealt with appropriately?

Class Projects to Enhance Community

As former President Bill Clinton has noted, "Almost everyone, regardless of income, available time, age, and skills, can do something useful for others and in the process, strengthen the fabric of our shared community."[4] As members of a caring classroom community, students can work together to help others by picking up litter around the school, working with younger children as buddies or tutors, making posters to draw attention to an issue or problem, raising money for a good cause, or recycling. An example of a project to enhance the classroom community is Kindness is Contagious.

Kindness is Contagious
Sheila Broyles

Students make posters encouraging people to be kind. The posters are placed throughout the community. Anyone can sign if they are willing to do an act of kindness. The kindergarteners enjoy estimating how many signatures they will get on the posters and sharing stories of the kind things they have done. In the month of February, 2010, our posters received 1,074 signatures.

Summary

To continue to realize the benefits of a classroom community, the teacher must plan activities to maintain and enhance the effectiveness of the classroom community. Regular opportunities for students to continue to get to know more about each other and to form friendships is one way this occurs.

In any community with limited resources, conflict will inevitably occur. Rather than treating conflict as a problem, effective teachers use conflict as an opportunity to teach problem solving skills and to help children learn to manage conflict effectively.

Class projects can also enhance the effectiveness of the classroom community. When students have opportunities to be of service to others in the school and in the community outside the school, group cohesion and team spirit is nurtured.

Footnotes

[1] Adapted from an activity in Lyman, L., Foyle, H. C., & Azwell, T. S. (1993). *Cooperative Learning in the Elementary Classroom.* Washington, DC: National Education Association, p. 48.
[2] Adapted from an activity in Lyman, Foyle, & Azwell, p. 49-50.
[3] Adapted from an activity in Lyman, Foyle, & Azwell, p. 50.
[4] Clinton, B. (2007). *Giving: How Each of Us Can Change the World.* New York, NY: Knopf.

Chapter Six
Utilizing Collaborative and Cooperative Learning

"Today at school we got assigned to reading groups. They don't come right out and tell you if you're in the Gifted group or the Easy group, but you can figure it out right away by looking at the covers of the books they hand out. I was pretty disappointed to find out I got put in the Gifted group, because that just means a lot of extra work."

Diary of a Wimpy Kid
Jeff Kinney, Amulet Books, 2007

Why It Is Important That Students Learn to Collaborate and Cooperate with Others

1. Students need to collaborate and cooperate with others to build and sustain friendships.

2. Students need to collaborate and cooperate with other students to work together on learning tasks in the classroom.

3. Students need to collaborate and cooperate with others to share resources.

4. Students need to collaborate and cooperate with others to manage conflicts and disagreements.

5. Students need to collaborate and cooperate with others to be successful in their relationships with peers and adults at school and outside of school.

6. Students will need to collaborate and cooperate to be successful in the world of work.

7. Students will need to collaborate and cooperate to be successful in marriage and parenting.

Opportunities for Collaboration and Cooperation in the Classroom

Elementary and middle school classrooms provide many opportunities for students to work together. Group building, which was discussed in a previous chapter, relies on positive interaction among students to help them get acquainted, to promote a positive classroom climate, and to practice needed academic and social skills, especially at the beginning of the school year. Group building activities should be used in an on-going basis throughout the year to continue to build a cooperative classroom community. Group building activities can also be used to help to teach social skills and to celebrate successful collaboration and cooperation.

At the beginning of class, students who have completed their assigned homework can be given time to go over their assignments to check their answers. If answers disagree, the students can attempt to reach agreement in the time provided. Students may change or correct their answers if they choose to do so. A reward for working together efficiently is that students will be able to check more work in the given time.

At the beginning of a lesson, a collaborative or cooperative learning activity can be used to review previous learning or skills that will be used during an upcoming lesson. Students can work together to practice a needed skill. The teacher can also use collaboration or cooperation to focus the students or build interest at the beginning of a lesson.

During a lesson, collaborative or cooperative learning activities can be used to provide a change of pace from the strategy the teacher has been using. Working together can provide opportunities to check the students' understanding of what they are learning or to practice a needed skill. A collaborative or cooperative assignment is an excellent way for the teacher to provide guided practice to the students.

At the end of class, a collaborative or cooperative activity can provide an opportunity for closure. The teacher may have the students work together to review the learning that has taken place during the lesson. By monitoring the groups as they work together, the teacher may check the group's understanding of the learning that has taken place and make appropriate decisions about where to begin during the next lesson.

Essential Conditions for Collaboration and Cooperation

Successful collaboration and cooperation do not occur by chance. In another chapter, the importance of a well-structured classroom environment in which students feel emotionally and physically safe was discussed. This environment is especially important when students are expected to interact positively and productively with each other in groups.

Group building, described in a previous chapter, must take place in order for students to become acquainted with each other and to learn about working together. Appropriate use of group building activities can help to meet students' needs for belonging, for power, for freedom, and for fun. Teachers need to use group building activities to analyze how well the students interact with each other and plan to teach needed skills for getting along and communicating in groups.

Competition in the classroom needs to be reduced or eliminated. Students are less likely to work together collaboratively and cooperatively if they view their peers as rivals. Activities which label students as "winners" and "losers," do not encourage collaboration and cooperation.

Students need to understand why they are working together and how it benefits them. It should be clear to the students that collaborative and cooperative activities provide needed practice on learning objectives. Through group discussion, the teacher can help students to be aware that some students learn better in groups and that most students find well-structured group activities enjoyable.

If concern about collaborative or cooperative learning activities is expressed by parents or family members or the teacher anticipates such concerns may occur, the teacher will want to provide information for family members about how he or she uses collaborative and cooperative learning and how these strategies benefit their students. This brochure and other National Education Association parent resources, provide information for parents (*Cooperative Learning: What You Need to Know*).

Problems with Group Grading

Giving a collaborative or cooperative group a shared grade for a learning activity is advocated by some educators. It is the position of the authors of this text that group grading should never be used for collaborative or cooperative activities. Working together with others should never cause harm to any member of the group and grades are very important to some students.

Group grading can promote anxiety among high achieving students who are highly motivated to do well in school. They may legitimately feel that they would have been more productive and efficient and that their grade would have been better had they been allowed to work individually. These feelings, in turn, may cause resentment of lower achieving learners or those less motivated to work in groups, frustrating efforts to encourage students to work together.

Group grading can cause considerable concern among parents who do not want their child to be penalized for working with others. Many parents want their child's grade to reflect his or her individual effort and to serve as an assessment of the student's individual work and progress.

Teachers can encourage students to work together by using group rewards other than grading. If the students' needs for belonging, power, freedom, and fun are met by working together, they will be motivated to collaborate and cooperate on other activities.

A complaint that students often make about working together is that some students contribute little to the group while others do most of the work. Grades should be the result of individual assessment which is an accurate gauge of the progress the individual student is making and the effort he or she put forth on the learning task. Students should not be penalized for working together collaboratively and cooperatively with others, nor should students who are not productive be rewarded by sharing a grade for work they have not contributed to.

Components of Collaborative and Cooperative Learning[1]

Positive interdependence is created by the way the teacher structures the activity so that students pull together to learn. Each group member must feel that he or she should actively participate and contribute for the group to be successful. Positive interdependence can encourage student motivation as learners feel responsible for working with the members of their group on the learning task. Providing a single copy of a learning resource, setting time limits, observing the students while they work together, and giving feedback are all strategies for promoting positive interdependence.

One of the best ways to promote positive interdependence is to give each member of the group a job or role to do which is related to the learning task. When assigning roles, the teacher should emphasize that each student is responsible for working on the learning task in addition to doing their assigned role. Jobs or roles are chosen to fit the learning task. For example, if younger students are working in pairs, as the teacher distributes materials to the pair, one student could be the 'counter' who makes sure the pair has the correct number of items. The other students could be the 'sorter' who makes sure the items are arranged or sequenced appropriately for the task.

Common Roles for Collaborative and Cooperative Tasks

Facilitator – keeps the group moving and makes sure all participate

Gofer – responsible for getting materials for the group as needed

Writer – writes or records the ideas of the group

Encourager – says positive things about other group member's contributions

Reporter – shares the group's ideas or answers with other groups or the class

---

Specialized roles may be created for specific subject areas or for particular learning tasks. There are a number of possible group roles for working with literature and for a social science report on a state or country.

"Lyman Describing Student Roles – Helper, Writer, Checker"

Group interaction occurs when the students are actively involved in the task. Active involvement can reduce management problems and promote for effective and efficient learning. As students work together, the teacher needs to be alert for social skills with which the students are having difficulty. Communication skills may also affect the way in which groups function. The ability to solve problems and manage conflict in a group is also needed if groups are to function productively. By observing the students as they work together, the teacher can identify the social, communication, and problem solving skills. The teacher provides feedback to the students as they are working and following the group activity.

"Students Working Together in Cooperative Groups"

Group processing helps students "debrief" after group activities. Group processing is designed to have the students reflect on what went well in the group. Goals for improving group work during future collaborative and cooperative experiences can also be discussed.

Group processing for young students may involve a nonverbal signal. Following a group activity, the teacher may demonstrate "I did all of the job." (hands wide apart) "I did some of the job." (hands apart) "I didn't do any of the job." (hands together) When the signals are understood, the teacher tells the students to close their eyes and hold their hands out to show how much of the job they did in the group activity. The teacher tells the students to hold their hands in place and open their eyes. This provides visual feedback of how each student feels he or she participated in the group. The teacher can talk with the class or with individuals about doing more or less of the group task next time.

Questions for group processing could include the following:

"What Made It Easy to Work in Your Group?"

"What Made It Easy to Work on the Task Together?"

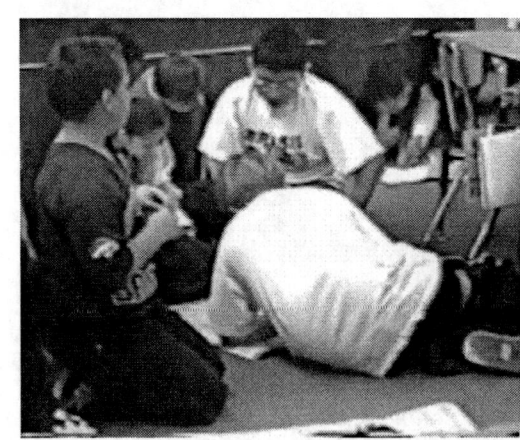

> **Additional Group Processing Questions**
>
> What did you learn from this activity?
>
> What is another example?
>
> How would you use this idea?
>
> What did you enjoy about the activity
>
> What is one way your group worked well together?
>
> Next time, what is one thing your group could work on?

The group may be given a sheet to guide its discussion of its work together and to record its self-assessment to share with the teacher. Skills assessed may vary according to the expectations for each task.

To facilitate group processing, a student in the group may be given the role of 'marker'. The marker is responsible for checking to see that each group member does his or her role during the task and completing the marker sheet at the end of the lesson. A marker check sheet could be given to the marker in each group.

The teacher may also use a recording sheet for each group as he or she observes the group as it works on the task. The teacher moves from group to group. Tally marks record each time the designated action is observed. The teacher should emphasize that he or she may not see every action performed by a group member since he or she has not observed the group for the whole time they were working together.

The teacher can use the recorder sheet to provide feedback to groups as they are working. After the task is completed, the teacher can provide a summary of his or her observations to the class or meet briefly with each group to give feedback. The teacher may want to have a brief conversation with any group members who did not appear to be actively participating in the group. There are other variations of group processing.

Individual accountability is an important part of any collaborative or cooperative activity. Because the students have worked together on a particular learning task, the work required of the individual following the group activity may be shorter in length than if the student had worked by himself or herself. Students must feel they are responsible for active participation in their groups and that they will be held accountable for their learning.

Group reward helps students to recognize the benefits of working together. The group reward may be something tangible, but if a tangible reward is used, it is important that all groups be able to earn the reward. If a group loses its reward because of the actions or performance of an individual group member, frustration or resentment may make future collaborative and cooperative activities more difficult.

Well-structured group activities provide intrinsic rewards by meeting students' needs for belonging, power, freedom, and fun. When the activity is fun and enjoyable, often no additional reward is needed. When groups can identify ways in which they worked together productively, this sense of shared accomplishment is often rewarding.

"Cooperative Group Reward – Sunflower Twinkie Design"

Positive feedback from the teacher can also be rewarding to students. When the teacher lets the students know how well they have worked together or how well they have done on the learning task, this feedback can serve as a reward.

Success is a component of productive collaborative and cooperative activities. Students need to feel that the group's work together has gone well. This is another reason why group building activities which promote success be used at the beginning of the year. When group activities are frustrating for group members, collaboration and cooperation in future activities may be more difficult.

Expectations for Students When Collaborating and Cooperating

Getting to know the members of the class

Getting ideas and information from other group members

Helping other group members by sharing ideas and information

Actively listening, sharing, and participating in the group

Encouraging other group members to actively share and participate

Being positive and enthusiastic about working together

Differences Between Collaborative Learning and Cooperative Learning

Collaborative learning involves students in working together. In collaborative learning, groups may be random or chosen by the students. In cooperative learning, groups are selected by the teacher, and students are grouped heterogeneously.

Many students may prefer to choose their own groups for collaborative learning activities. However, when students choose their groups, there are several disadvantages. Students who are not chosen by others may feel left out. This feeling interferes with the student's needs for acceptance and belonging and works against the goal of promoting a classroom community.

When students choose their own groups or when groups are chosen at random, students of the same ability level may end up working together. For high achieving students, this can result in on-task behavior and excellent group products. However, some high achieving students may not get along with each other in groups, competing for the leadership of the group in unproductive ways.

When there are student-chosen groups or random groups that result in students with lower academic and social skills being grouped together, problems with the productivity of the group are likely to occur. Students may be off-task, may not relate well to each other, or may not have the skills to help each other accomplish the group task.

An obvious disadvantage of random student groups is that students who do not get along together may inadvertently be in the same group. This may result in unproductive conflict or off-task behavior.

When students are grouped together by the teacher, careful consideration can be given to the students in each group. Heterogeneous grouping of students by the teacher is one of the important components of cooperative learning that distinguishes cooperative learning from collaborative learning or 'group work'.

Heterogeneous Grouping of Students for Cooperative Learning

When grouping for cooperative learning, the achievement of the students is one of the important considerations for placing students in groups. As opposed to ability grouping, grouping by achievement is based on the actual performance of the students in the particular subject area. Groups can be more flexible as student achievement related to a particular skill may not be consistent with their usual performance.

Heterogeneous grouping may also take into account the gender, ethnicity, and the socioeconomic status of the students. The goal of heterogeneous grouping is 'max mix'. Mixed groups have the greatest potential for success in cooperative learning, because student differences provide opportunities for greater student interaction in the groups.[2]

"Strategies for Forming Classroom Groups"

Benefits of Cooperative Learning

Cooperative learning has academic and social benefits for the student and for the teacher that have been verified by research. (Azwell, et. al., 1999, Johnson & Johnson, 1994, Lyman & Foyle, 2007, Slavin, 1990)[3] When cooperative learning is used appropriately, students achieve academically at higher levels. Students also gain socially when appropriately involved in cooperative learning groups. Some of the social benefits of cooperative learning include: higher levels of student self-esteem, growth in social skills, increased liking of school, and increased liking for other students.

Steps in Implementing Cooperative Learning

1. The content to be taught is identified and appropriate criteria for mastery by the students using the appropriate curriculum standards.

2. The most useful cooperative learning strategy is identified by the teacher. Group size is determined based on the cooperative skills of the students and the strategy selected.

3. Students are assigned to heterogeneous groups.

4. The classroom is arranged to facilitate group interaction.

5. Group processes are taught or reviewed as needed to assure that groups will run smoothly.

6. The teacher clarifies expectations for group learning to the students and makes sure they understand the reasons why they are working together. A time line for the cooperative activity is made clear to the students.

7. The teacher presents the initial content material, using appropriate instructional strategies.

8. While the groups are working together, the teacher monitors student interaction in the groups.
   The teacher provides assistance and clarification as needed. The teacher reviews group skills as needed and provides positive feedback to groups who are working together effectively. The teacher facilitates problem solving with groups who are not working together effectively.

9. Learning outcomes are evaluated. Students must individually demonstrate that they understand the concepts or skills.

10. Groups are rewarded for success. Verbal recognition by the teacher, recognition in a class newsletter, and recognition on a bulletin board are examples of ways to celebrate group success.[4]

Social and Communication Skills

To successfully implement cooperative learning, the teacher needs to help students to acquire, to refine, and to actively use social and communication skills. These skills can be taught and practiced while students are interacting in cooperative learning groups.[5]

For example, students will need to share a variety of materials with one another and among each other within groups. Students must learn to use appropriate voice levels when they are working together. Students must actively listen to one another in order to share and discuss ideas within the group. Students can assist each other as they are learning these skills.

While they are working together, students are encouraged to accept each other. During disagreements, students can be taught how to manage conflict and how to express differing ideas and opinions constructively. These skills are taught by the teacher and reinforced by the teacher and by group members as the students are working together. As students become more proficient in using social skills, they are able to apply those skills in interactions outside the classroom.

Further examples of psychosocial and interpersonal life skills are provided by UNICEF and the following table.

Examples of Social Skills	Examples of Communication Skills
Saying please and thank you	Actively listening to others
Staying on task	Using appropriate voices
Encouraging others	Positive nonverbal behavior
Disagreeing without hurting other's feelings	Asking questions
Being positive and constructive	Clarifying the instructions
Making eye contact with others	Repeating other's ideas and paraphrasing
Keeping hands and feet controlled	Giving reasons for your ideas
Conflict management	Identifying areas of agreement
Making sure everyone is included	Reaching agreement
Respecting individual differences	Brainstorming ideas and strategies

Boys and Girls Town is an organization that focuses on building relationships and teaching/modeling social skills through positive interactions with students. Some examples of social skills that they focus on is disagreeing appropriately, getting the teacher's attention, and disagreeing appropriately. It is imperative that students are taught and practice appropriate social skills so that they can work cooperatively and productively with adults and other students.

Teaching Social Skills

As students are working together, the teacher can observe the groups to identify social and communication skills that are needed. Teachers also need to identify observable behaviors that demonstrate success in using the skill. For example, if the teacher has observed that students need to encourage each other as they are working together, the teacher can ask students to suggest words or phrases that are encouraging. It is important to have the students generate some of the examples so that the examples use words that are familiar to them. Student ideas can be recorded on a T Chart.

T Chart

Skill _____

Sounds like	Does not sound like
Looks like	Does not look like

After the teacher records the students' ideas on the T chart, the teacher can present a cooperative learning task and ask students to encourage at least one other student as they are working on the task. The teacher will be walking around while the students are working to provide feedback about how well the students are applying the skill. As the teacher listens to the groups, he or she may see or hear positive examples of ideas that can be added to the T Chart.

The T chart can be displayed on an electronic white board or on a piece of chart paper so that it can be reused and referred to as the students are practicing the skill. It is important to note that students do not necessarily master a skill without a number of opportunities for practice. Having charts available for display of the skills that the students are working on can help the students use the skills more effectively.

When the students are finished working on the cooperative task, the group processing can include having students share examples of positive things they heard or saw while they were working together. This process may need to be repeated during several work sessions in order for a particular social skill to be used appropriately by the students. It will also be necessary to review a particular skill from time to time.

Examples of Cooperative Learning Strategies

There are a number of cooperative learning strategies (as noted by Prince George's County Public Schools in *A Guide to Cooperative Learning*) that vary in terms of grade level, groupings of students, and objectives for the strategy. These cooperative learning structures promote social skills and community building.

Think Pair Share was developed by Frank Lyman, Jr. It is one of the easiest cooperative learning strategies to implement and works well with both younger and older students.

CUEING	agreed on signals for switching student response modes	teacher's voice wall chart hand signal
THINKING	hands-down pause between the teacher's question and the pair or share mode	unstructured thinking cognitive mapping defending
PAIRING	sharing, discussing, and problem solving between assigned pairs of students	unstructured active listening (tell partner's answer) consensus
SHARING	selected students share their responses from the pair mode	pairs share with whole class Think-Pair-Square Think-Pair-Square-Share

Lyman, F. (1992). *Think Pair Share.* Washington, DC: National Education Association. Videotape.

One popular and effective variation of *Think, Pair, Share* is *Think, Write, Pair, Share*. This strategy adds the step of students writing down their own response after they have had adequate time to think. This can increase individual student accountability and ensure that both partners have something to share when it is time to pair. When students are discussing with their partner, they have the option of changing their written response when appropriate. Another variation is *Think, Pair, Square, Share*. This strategy works well when students are seated in groups of four. When students are prompted to square, the two pairs that are seated at the table will discuss their responses before answers are shared with the entire group. This allows students to hear more students' perspectives and helps encourage participation from students who are more comfortable sharing in smaller groups. As with any cooperative learning strategy, the goal is that students are positively interacting with one another, and the interaction enhances and deepens their understanding of that concept.

"Think Pair Share Activity – Upper Grade Classroom"

Student Teams-Achievement Divisions (STAD) was developed by Robert Slavin and promotes individual student achievement. An advantage of the strategy is that it allows the classroom teacher to use the same instructional strategies as he or she has previously used. Assessments generally do not need to change. Teams work together on the assignment and are tested individually.

Teams – Games – Tournaments (TGT), also developed by Robert Slavin, is like STAD but includes a competitive tournament which can be used for practice before the individual assessment takes place. Further information is found in Slavin, R. E. (1994). *A Practical Guide to Cooperative Learning.* Upper Saddle River, NJ: Prentice Hall.

The *Jigsaw Classroom* is a cooperative learning strategy developed by Eliot Aronson to promote better learning and reduce conflict in the classroom.

Spencer Kagan's *Simple structures* or *Kagan Structures* promote cooperation by using a number of different strategies. *Showdown* is seen in Mrs. Agnew's Third Grade Classroom. *Numbered Heads Together* is demonstrated in <u>Mrs. Hine's Second Grade classroom</u>.

"Mrs. Agnew's Third Grade Classroom (*Showdown*)"

"Mrs. Hine's Second Grade Classroom (*Numbered Heads Together*)"

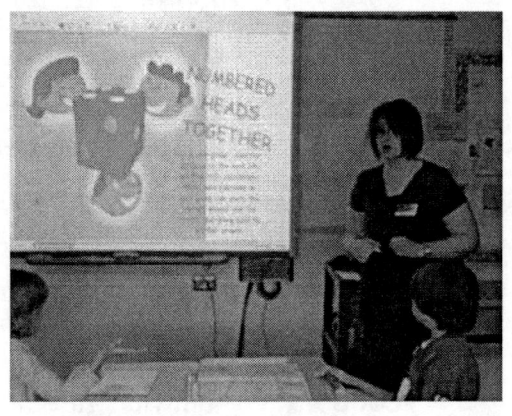

"Numbered Heads Together Activity – Upper Grade Classroom"

Other Cooperative Learning structures include the following ones.

Peer-Assisted Learning promotes positive learning effects when students who are learning English work together in peer-assisted learning.

Roger T. Johnson and David W. Johnson have well-researched approaches for cooperative learning approaches that emphasize social skills.

Tribes Learning Community is another approach to collaborative and cooperative learning. It is designed to promote caring communities of children.

Strategies for Assessing Cooperative Learning

When assessing the outcomes of cooperative learning, teachers need to assess both group and individual achievement. Some general approaches that can be used to assess collaborative and cooperative learning:

1. ***Teacher observation.*** Teacher observation is one form of assessment that is particularly appropriate for younger learners. The teacher may use notes, student marker sheets, or teacher marker sheets.

2. ***Group observation.*** Group members may help to assess their own progress as part of a group processing activity, in a written activity, or using an observation sheet.

3. ***Group product.*** The teacher and students assess the quality of the group's product. Rubrics may be helpful.

4. ***Individual assessment.*** Each collaborative or cooperative activity needs to have some form of individual assessment. This individual assessment is appropriate for grading purposes.

Teachers who are just beginning to implement collaborative and cooperative activities in their classrooms should keep their usual process for grading individual students. Teachers with more experience using collaboration and cooperation may choose to utilize several of the assessment strategies in combination to assess student learning.

Troubleshooting with Collaborative and Cooperative Learning

1. Problems can occur when implementing any instructional strategy. Collaborative and cooperative learning can be particularly challenging to implement with older students who have not had opportunities to practice collaborating and cooperating in previous classrooms. For these students, it is especially important for the students to understand why they are being asked to work together.

2. Students may need instruction and practice in social and communication skills in order to be successful with collaborative and cooperative learning.

3. Group grading is unproductive and may cause unnecessary anxiety among students and parents.

4. Don't overuse collaborative and cooperative learning strategies. Students need to have opportunities to work on their own and to learn with other instructional approaches as well.

5. Be sure that the students' initial experiences with collaborative and cooperative learning provide success for the students.

6. Collaborative and cooperative learning strategies work best in a classroom community. Continue to work on building and sustaining the classroom community throughout the school year.

7. Some collaborative and cooperative structures may not work well with some student groups. Try different structures to meet the developmental needs of your students.

8. While observing student interaction in groups, be alert to verbal and nonverbal signals that students are upset or unhappy. Individual or group conferences with the students can help to address concerns that the students have. If most of the class is upset or unhappy about working together, a class meeting can be used to discuss the concerns as a class.

9. Sometimes too much collaboration and cooperation is expected to occur too quickly. Introducing the skills needed for working together more slowly and sequentially.

10. High achieving students may feel they are being asked to do all of the work for their group or that they are being penalized for working with other students. Stress positive interdependence and reassure the students that they will not be adversely affected by working with others.

11. Parents and family members may be concerned about collaborative and cooperative learning. Use back to school night and class newsletters as ways to explain the benefits of collaborative and cooperative learning. Make sure family members understand that you are using collaborative and cooperative learning as a strategy to practice skills and ideas. Students will be assessed and graded individually based on their own progress and effort.

12. When implementing any new instructional strategy, use lots of positive feedback and encouragement with students. Patience and persistence will pay off.

Summary

Collaborative and cooperative learning are building blocks of any interactive classroom. Positive interdependence, group processing, group interaction, individual accountability, and success are components of successful collaborative and cooperative learning activities. Even though collaborative and cooperative learning are valid instructional strategies, any strategy can be overused.

Although positive benefits are likely to be seen with both collaborative and cooperative learning, the research proven benefits of improved academic achievement, improved attitudes, and improved liking of school and of peers are found in heterogeneous cooperative groups chosen by the teacher.

Additional Resources

Cohen, E. G. (1994). *Designing Groupwork: Strategies for the Heterogeneous Classroom.* New York, NY: Teachers College Press.

Ellis, S. S., & Whalen, S. F. (1996). *Cooperative Learning: Getting Started.* New York, NY: Scholastic Professional Books.

Foyle, H. C., & Lyman, L. (2007). *Cooperative Learning: Engaging Students.* Scotts Valley, CA: Create Space. DVD.

Foyle, H. C., & Lyman, L. (2007). *Cooperative Learning: Grouping for Interactive Learning.* Scotts Valley, CA: Create Space. DVD.

Foyle, H. C. (ed., 1995). *Interactive Learning in the Higher Education Classroom: Cooperative, Collaborative, and Active Learning Strategies.* Washington, DC: National Education Assn.

Foyle, H. C. (1992, Spring). Who Killed JFK? A Group Investigation. *Cooperative Learning, 12* (3), 42-44.

Gillies, R. M. (2007). *Cooperative Learning: Integrating Theory and Practice.* Thousand Oaks, CA: Sage Publications.

Johnson, D. W., Johnson, R. T., & Holubec, E. J. (1994). *The New Circles of Learning: Cooperation in the Classroom and School.* Alexandria, VA: Association for Supervision and Curriculum Development.

Lyman, L., & Foyle, H. C. (1990, Spring). The Constitution in Action: A Cooperative Learning Approach. *Georgia Social Science Journal, 21* (1), 24-34.

Lyman, L., & Foyle, H. C. (1990). *Cooperative Grouping for Interactive Learning: Students, Teachers, and Administrators.* Washington, DC: National Education Association.

Lyman, L., & Foyle, H. C. (1991, September-October). Teaching Geography Using Cooperative Learning. *Journal of Geography, 90* (5), 223-226.

Sapon-Shevin. M. (1998). *Because We Can Change the World: A Practical Guide to Building Cooperative, Inclusive Classroom Communities.* Boston: Allyn and Bacon.

Sharan, S. (ed., 1999). *Handbook of Cooperative Learning Methods.* Westport, CT: Praeger.

Shulman, J. H., Lotan, R. A., & Whitcomb, J. A. (1998). *Groupwork in Diverse Classrooms.* New York, NY: Teachers College Press.

Williams, R. B. (2007). *Cooperative Learning: A Standard for High Achievement.* Thousand Oaks, CA: Sage Publication.

Footnotes

[1] Foyle, H. C., Lyman, L., & Thies, S. A. (1991). *Cooperative Learning in the Early Childhood Classroom.* Washington, DC: National Education Association, pp. 16-18, 36-38.

[2] Lyman, L., Foyle, H. C., & Azwell, T. S. (1993). *Cooperative Learning in the Elementary Classroom.* Washington, DC: National Education Association, p. 31.

[3] Azwell, T. S., et.al., (1999). *Constructing Curriculum in Context.* Dubuque, IA: Kendall/Hunt, p. 407-410; Johnson, D. W., & Johnson, R. T. (1994). *Learning Together and Alone: Cooperative, Competitive, and Individualistic Learning* (4th ed.). Boston: Allyn and Bacon; Lyman, L., & Foyle, H. C. (2007). *Cooperative Learning: Engaging Students.* Scotts Valley, CA: Create Space. DVD; Slavin, R. E. (1990). *Cooperative Learning: Theory, Research, and Practice* (2nd ed.). Boston: Allyn and Bacon.

[4] Lyman, L., & Foyle, H. C. (2007). *Cooperative Learning: Engaging Students.* Scotts Valley, CA: Create Space. DVD.

[5] Lyman, L., Foyle, H. C., & Azwell, T. S. (1993). *Cooperative Learning in the Elementary Classroom.* Washington, DC: National Education Association, pp. 39-40.

Chapter Seven
Activities for Collaborative and Cooperative Learning Lessons

'A grower of turnips or a shaper of clay,
a…farmer or a king – every man is a hero if he strives
more for others than for himself alone.'

Taran in *The High King*
by Lloyd Alexander, Yearling, 1968

When planning a cooperative learning lesson, teachers can use the following template to build the lesson. As with any lesson plan format, not all of the steps will necessarily be included for each lesson, but teachers need to think about why they may choose not to include a particular step as they are planning. The steps that must be included in each cooperative lesson plan are:

Essential Steps for All Cooperative Learning Lesson Plans

Objective
Materials needed
Procedure
Group processing (group assessment)
Individual accountability (individual assessment)

"Planning Cooperative Learning Groups"

In the examples which follow the template, the activities can be adapted to a wide variety of content and grade levels. Examples of the Kansas social studies standards have been added to two of the lessons, but teachers will need to align lesson activities with the appropriate curriculum standards for their district or state and grade levels.

Cooperative Learning Lesson Plan Template

Title or topic of the lesson	
Standard or standards	
Objective	
Materials needed for the lesson	
Group skill to work on	
Roles	
Procedure	
Group processing (group assessment)	
Group reward	
Individual accountability	

Assembly Line

1909 Ford Model T
National Automobile Museum
Reno, Nevada

Standard: Kansas Department of Education, Social Studies, 4th Grade Economics, Benchmark 2, Personal Financial Literacy
The student defines the characteristics of an entrepreneur and gives an example of someone who shows those characteristics (e. g., risk taker, innovator, gets together all resources needed to produce a product).

Website: Kansas State Board of Education. (2004). *Kansas Standards for History and Government; Economics and Geography*, p. 115. Retrieved from http://www.ksde.org/Default.aspx?tabid=1678

Objective: Students will identify the characteristics of Henry Ford that made him an entrepreneur.

Materials: Copy of the poem The Assembly Line"[1] for each group, copy of individual assessment for each student
Plastic glove for each student
Vanilla wafers, chocolate cookies, red and yellow frosting
Napkin for each student

Group Skill to Work On: Using appropriate voice levels, staying on task

Roles: Reader – reads the poem to the group
Writer – writes the group's answers
Reporter – shares the group's answers with the class when asked to do so.

Procedure: The teacher groups the students in heterogeneous groups of 3 or 4.
In groups, students will read the poem 'The Assembly Line'. Each group will answer the questions about the poem. Roles: Reader, reads the poem to the group; Writer, writes the group's answers; Reporter, shares the group's answers with the class when asked to do so.

1. What was different about Henry Ford's assembly line?
2. What did Billy's father like about working on the assembly line?
3. What did Billy's father not like about working on the assembly line.

The teacher explains the assembly line procedure for making a cookie sandwich.

Worker # 1 starts with the bottom bun (vanilla wafer) and places cookie burger chocolate cookie)

Worker # 2 asks the customer if they want ketchup (red frosting)

Worker # 3 asks the customer if they want mustard (yellow frosting)

Worker # 4 (worker # 3 for 3 person groups) places top bun on the product and thanks the customer.

Two groups at a time participate in the assembly line. The groups alternate the roles of assembly line workers and customers. If desired, each group of workers can make extra cookies to share with the principal, counselor, secretary, custodian, nurse, music teacher, physical education teacher, and others as appropriate.

While groups are participating in the assembly line activity, other groups read an assigned article (web site link) and identify the characteristics that made the person an entrepreneur.

Website link: Two American Entrepreneurs: Madam C. J. Walker and J. C. Penney

Group processing: Each group shares one way its members worked well together. Teacher provides positive feedback about his or her observations of how the groups stayed on task and used appropriate voice levels.

Group reward: Cookies to eat

Individual accountability: Students answer the following questions:
1. How did you feel about working on the assembly line?
2. What did Henry Ford do that made him an entrepreneur?
3. What was one good thing about the assembly line, according to the poem?
4. What was one bad thing about the assembly line, according to the poem?

Change for a Quarter[2]

Objective: Students will identify possible coin combinations that add up to 25 cents.

Grouping: Students are grouped in heterogeneous groups of 2, 3, or 4, depending on the class' skill in cooperating.

Roles: Writer – writes down the combinations the group thinks of
Reporter – shares the group's ideas with the class when told to do so
For larger groups, one or more students may be given the role of encourager, to say at least one positive thing to each group member as the group is working.

Group skill to work on: Use of appropriate voice levels in groups, encouraging

Procedure: The teacher reviews the use of appropriate voice levels in the group then asks students to model ways of encouraging group members to share ideas. The groups are given the task of determining how many different combinations of coins they can come up with that will equal exactly 25 cents. The teacher monitors the groups as they are working, giving feedback about how well the groups are using appropriate voice levels and encouraging each other. When the students are finished, the teacher has the groups take turns sharing answers they have thought of. It is helpful to list the responses on the smart board so the groups will know which answers have already been given.

Group processing: Each student should say something positive to his or her group members about working together. The teacher can suggest starting with "I like the way we ..." as a prompt for students.

Answers: ( ) denotes a coin value

1 (25)	5 (5)	25 (1)
1(5), 20 (1)	2 (5), 15 (1)	3 (5), 10 (1)
4 (5), 5 (1)	1 (5), 2 (10)	3 (5), 1 (10)
15 (1), 1 (10)		5 (1), 2 (10)
10 (1), 1 (5), 1 (10)		5 (1), 2 (5), 1 (10)

Individual Accountability: Students tell whether the following combinations equal exactly 25 cents.

1. 2 (10), 1 (5)   (Answer = yes)

2. 3 (5), 2(1)   (Answer = no)

3. 5 (1), 1 (10), 2 (5)   (Answer = yes)

4. 1 (10), 2 (5), 5 (1)   (Answer = yes)

5. 3 (5), 1 (10), 5 (1)   (Answer = no)

Web site: Change Maker Game   www.funbrain.com/cashreg/

Colorful Language[3]

Objective: Students will identify colorful verbs that could be used for given sports teams.

Materials: Worksheet for each group

Grouping: Heterogeneous groups of three or four

Procedure: The teacher tells the students that good writers use colorful, expressive language to interest readers in their stories. For example, a sportswriter might write that the Dallas Cowboys were *stampeded* by a team they lost to in a football game. Working with their groups, the students will match the given verbs to the appropriate sports team. The groups will then create a colorful verb for a given team.

<u>**Verbs to Use**</u>

bucked	deviled	dethroned	dirtied
dulled	eclipsed	extinguished	grounded
handcuffed	scuttled	shrunk	stalled
sunk	tamed	tangled	

In their recent loss,

1. the Detroit Lions were _____.

2. the Los Angeles Kings were _____.

3. the Denver Broncos were _____.

4. the Seattle Mariners were _____.

5. the Tampa Bay Buccaneers were _____.

6. the Pittsburgh Steelers were _____.

7. the Phoenix Suns were _____.

8. the Chicago White Sox were _____.

9. the New York Jets were _____.

10. the San Francisco Giants were _____.

11. the New Orleans Saints were _____.

12. the New Jersey Nets were _____.

13. the Buffalo Sabres were _____.

14. the Calgary Flames were _____.

15. the San Diego Chargers were _____.

As a group, decide on a colorful verb to describe the loss of the following teams.

16. the Florida Gators were _____.

17. the Eastern Kentucky Colonels were _____.

18. the Massachusetts Minutemen were _____.

Individual Accountability: Students will match the verbs with the appropriate teams.

Words to Use
axed bitten plucked stoned stung

1. The Georgia Bulldogs were _____.

2. The Colorado Rockies were _____.

3. The Emporia State Hornets were _____.

4. The Delaware Fightin' Blue Hens were _____.

5. The Indiana State Sycamores were _____.

Activity Answers

1. tamed
2. dethroned
3. bucked
4. sunk
5. grounded
6. handcuffed
7. eclipsed
8. dirtied
9. grounded
10. shrunk
11. deviled
12. tangled
13. dulled
14. extinguished
15. stalled

Individual Accountability
1. bitten
2. stoned
3. stung
4. plucked
5. axed

Website: Sports games for kids   www.sikids.com/games/

Faith and the Electric Dogs

Objective: Students will identify vocabulary words and idioms that are connected with positive and negative feelings.

Grouping: Heterogeneous groups of three or four

Materials: Copies of the book *Faith and the Electric Dogs* by Patrick Jennings (Scholastic, 1998), copy of the worksheet for each group

Roles: Writer – writes down the group's answers
Researcher – finds the vocabulary word in the text, reads text to group
Reporter – tells the group's answers to the class when asked to do so
Monitor – makes sure the group's noise level is appropriate
(in groups of three, the reporter is also the monitor)

Group skill to work on: Using appropriate voice levels

Procedure: The teacher displays the vocabulary words and the pages from the story on which the words can be found on the smart board. In their groups, students find the word in the text and write its meaning. Students may use dictionaries if they wish. After the students have looked up the words, the groups determine the meaning of phrases about events from the book.

Faith and the Electric Dogs

Writer _____   Researcher _____

Reporter _____   Monitor _____

obedient _____

dazzling _____

luscious _____

maddening _____

confounded _____

blissful _____

ominous _____

frustrated _____

Tell whether the person is *happy* or *unhappy*.

1. Bernice was *tickled pink* with her new home in Mexico.
   _____

2. Faith felt *blue* when Sr. Latas didn't understand her.
   _____

3. At first, Eddie was *yellow* about riding in Faith's rocket.
   _____

4. Bernice *saw red* when Hector let Eddie come into the house.
   _____

5. Faith was in a *gray* mood because of the cold, wet weather.
   _____

When the groups are finished, the teacher has the reporters from the groups share their group's answers with the class. If there is disagreement among the groups about an answer, the students reread the text to check their answer. When the group sharing has been completed, the students complete the individual accountability assignment.

Individual Accountability:

Faith and the Electric Dogs

Name _____

For each vocabulary word you studied with your group, put a ☺ if the word makes people happy, put a ☹ if the word makes people sad.

_____obedient

_____dazzling

_____luscious

_____maddening

_____confounded

_____blissful

_____ominous

_____frustrated

Eddie told Faith that he was *true blue*. What did he mean? _____

_____

_____

Patrick Jennings Amazon.com webpage

The Food Groups

Objective: Students will identify the food group each food from their school lunch menu belongs in.

Grouping: Students are grouped heterogeneously in groups of two or three.

Materials: Access to Food Pyramid website or copy of the Food Pyramid for each group.
Food pyramid is available at this website www.mypyramid.gov.

Group skill to work on: Agreeing and disagreeing constructively

Procedure: The teacher presents the Food Pyramid and gives the whole class opportunities to practice identifying the correct food group for foods.

Each group is given a copy of the actual lunch menu for their school for two days.

Monday's menu	Tuesday's menu
Lasagna Garlic bread Tater tots Corn Tropical fruit Milk	Sliced turkey Roll Mashed potatoes Gravy Green beans Fruited jello Holiday cookie Milk

The group identifies the correct food group for each food on the menu.

Two groups meet together to discuss their answers.

Using the Numbered Heads Together strategy, members of the two combined groups report answers to the class.

Group processing: The group will rate their group on the following criteria:

    We got the task done. ☺ ☹

    Everybody in the group helped. ☺ ☹

    We listened to each other. ☺ ☹

    We disagreed without hurting anyone's feelings. ☺ ☹

Individual Accountability: Students identify the correct food groups from a menu from another school day.

Wednesday's menu
Fish sticks
Oven fries
Carrots
Applesauce
Milk

How I Spent My Summer Vacation

Objective: Students will demonstrate comprehension of narrative text by correctly identifying which events from the story could have occurred in real life.

Materials: How I Spent My Summer Vacation by Marc Teague (Crown Publishers, 1995)
Copy of the story events sheet for each group

Grouping: Students are grouped in heterogeneous groups of two or three.

Roles: Writer – writes the group's answers
Reporter – reports the group's answers to the class
(for groups of three, two reporters take turns reporting answers)

Group skill to work on: Encouraging other group members – each group member will tell why they liked working with the other members of the group.

Procedure: The teacher reads the story to the class. After reading the story, the teacher shares individual pictures from the story with the class and asks the students whether the picture shows an event that really could have happened. The teacher asks the students what clues from the pictures show them that an event probably could not have happened.

Students work in their groups to decide whether events from the story could have occurred in real life.

Could the event from the story really have happened?

_____ 1. Wallace Bleff spent the summer in the West.

_____ 2. Wallace Bleff rode on a train during the summer.

_____ 3. Wallace stayed with his aunt.

_____ 4. The cowboys wanted the young boy to work with them.

_____ 5. Wallace could start a fire using sticks.

_____ 6. Wallace's aunt invited all the cowboys over for a picnic.

_____ 7. There was a band playing at the picnic.

_____ 8. Wallace used a tablecloth to frighten the cattle who were stampeding.

Groups report their answers to the class by having the reporter for each group signal the group's answer – thumbs up for an event that could have occurred in real life, thumbs down for an event that could not have occurred in real life.

Group Processing: Each group will share one thing they did well as a group when they worked together.

Individual accountability: Each student tells whether the following event from the story could have really happened. *Wallace brought a bull and a prairie dog to school for show and tell.*

Group building activity: Each student writes down three things he or she did in the past summer. Two should be true, one should be made up. The students get back with their groups and share the events from their summers. The group members try to identify the true events and the event that is not true.

Extending the activity: Students watch an interview with the author and tell how he gets ideas for his stories.

"Interview with Marc Teague"

Native American Dwellings of the Past[4]

Jody Drake

Objective: The students will investigate Native American dwellings, construct models, and make oral reports.

Materials: Social studies textbook, materials to construct the models

Roles: Reader – reads material from to the group
Note Taker – writes down the information the group learns
Checker – makes sure everyone understands what is read; that is, he or she asks for explanations in each group member's own words)

Procedure:

1. Each group selects a different historical Native American dwelling type (tepee, wigwam, longhouse, hogan, pueblo) to study.

2. Roles are chosen by the students in each group.

3. Groups study the appropriate portion of the social studies textbook together.

4. The groups research additional sources of information. Students switch roles.

5. Each group contributes a chapter with illustrations to the class book *Native American Dwellings of the Past* which is word processed.

6. The groups construct models of the dwellings with an emphasis on the equal contributions of group members. These projects can be displayed in the library along with the class book. A variety of materials can be used to build the models:

   wigwam (papier-mâché)

   tepee (cloth and sticks)

   longhouse (milk carton and toothpicks)

   hogan (dough that hardens)

   pueblo (construction paper, sand, toothpick ladders)

7. Each group can report to the class about the group's findings.

8. The major components of any body of knowledge (in this case, Native American dwellings) can be cooperatively investigated and reported using this approach. Content could be selected from any subject area (e. g. science, social studies, literature).

Individual accountability: Each student writes a brief report about how he or she helped the group with the assigned tasks.

Website: **National Museum of the American Indian**

The Solar System

Objective: Students will compare and contrast the planets in the Solar System.

Grouping: Students are heterogeneously grouped in groups of 3 or 4.

Materials: computers for group research, *Jeopardy!*™ style game for Smart Board, 3x5 index cards for tournament questions

Roles:
   Writer writes or types the information the group finds.
   Checker verifies that all questions are answered in the report.
   Reporter tells the information the group found out to the class.
   In groups of four, *two reporters* may share the responsibility for telling the information.

Group skill to work on: Staying on task

Procedure:

Brainstorming – Students create a list of things about the planets they would like to compare. As a group, the class may agree on questions like:

   What does the name of the planet mean?
   Which planets are closest to the Sun?
   Which planets are larger and smaller than Earth?
   Does the planet have any moons?
   What is the atmosphere of the planet?
   What is an interesting fact about the planet?
   Each group report must have information to answer each question.

Research – Using the websites below the students research the answers to the questions generated by the class.

Fact Monster
factmonster.com

Yahoo! Kids
kids.yahoo.com

Solar System Exploration
solarsystem.nasa.gov/planets/index.cfm

Sharing Information – Each group reports the information they have found. Each student makes an information sheet with the facts they learn.

Group Study – In their groups, the students study the information from the reports, quizzing each other to make sure all students know the information.

Review Game – Using information from the student reports, the teacher creates a Jeopardy style review game that the students will play in teams.

Template for *Jeopardy!*™ style game www.wfnss.ca/math/smart_board_resources.htm

Teams-Games-Tournaments – Students are grouped by the teacher in groups of three or four based on their achievement (grades) in science. High achievers will compete against each other, low achievers will compete against each other. Using information from the Jeopardy style review game, the teacher creates tournament cards for each group OR students write the cards using the information their research group found about their planet. Tournament cards (3 x 5) index cards work well) have a question on the front and the answer on the back. At the tournament tables, students take turns going first. First student to correctly answer the card keeps the card. If no one answers a card, it goes to the bottom of the pile to be played again. Students take their points from the tournament back to their original group. Results of the tournament may be posted by team.

Website **Suggestions for using Teams Games Tournaments can be found at www.accessexcellence.org/AE/AEPC/WWC/1995/tournaments.php**

Vanity License Plates[5]

Objective: Students will match given vanity license plates with their owners and create a personal license plate.

Materials: Copy of the worksheet and pattern for the individual license plate

Grouping: Groups of 3

Roles: Writer – writes the group's answers
Leader – asks the group members what they did well together at the end
Reporter – shares the group's answers with the class when asked to do so

Group skill to work on: Celebrating group success

Procedure: The teacher asks students if they have seen vanity license plates and asks why people choose to have vanity license plates. Students work in groups to match the license plates on the worksheet with their owners. After discussing the answers with the class, each group suggests one or two ideas for each group member to use in creating his or her own personal plate. Before the students work individually on their license plates, the leader asks the group members what they did well in working together and reports this to the class (if time permits).

YDRYV65	2DALOO	UPN ATM
AW SHUX	HOME RN	IN XTC
IM 4 JAKE	HRMYONE	YLEKYOT
2TH DR	NOV L T	H8 2 LUZ

_____ a very modest person

_____ a baseball fan

_____ someone who likes to travel

_____ a Harry Potter fan

_____	a very happy person
_____	a morning person
_____	a very competitive person
_____	an inventor
_____	a cartoon fan
_____	a dentist
_____	someone who likes to drive fast
_____	a *Twilight* fan

Activity answers:

AW SHUX	a very modest person	HOME RN	a baseball fan
2DALOO	someone who likes to travel	HRMYONE	a Harry Potter fan
IN XTC	a very happy person	UPN ATM	a morning person
H8 2 LUZ	a very competitive person	NOV L T	an inventor
YLEKYOT	a cartoon fan	2TH DR	a dentist
YDRYV65	someone who likes to drive fast	IM 4 JAKE	a *Twilight* fan

Individual accountability: Students create a personal license plate on a template. The plates are displayed on a class bulletin board and students try to decide who created each plate.

Harry Potter vanity license plates
www.mugglenet.com/plates.shtml

Which Would You Rather Be?

Standard: Kansas Department of Education, Social Studies, Kindergarten Economics, Benchmark 1, Limited Resources

The student understands that a person cannot have everything he/she *wants*, so a choice has to be made (e.g, play video games or watch television; play on swings or play soccer). The student explains what he/she gives up when a choice is made.

Teacher Notes: *Wants* – desires that can be satisfied by consuming a good, service, or leisure activity

Web site: Kansas State Board of Education. (2004). *Kansas Standards for History and Government; Economics and Geography*, p. 55. Retrieved from http://www.ksde.org/Default.aspx?tabid=1678

Objective: The student will choose between two items and tell what he or she gave up when the choice was made.

Materials: Copy of the book *Which Would You Rather Be?* (W. Steig and H. Bliss, HarperCollins Publishers, 2002), Individual response sheet for each student

Group skill to work on: Actively listening to your partner

Procedure: The teacher discusses wants and choices. Students use a 'left hand' or 'right hand' to signal which they prefer. The teacher calls on one student to tell what they gave up when they made their choice. The teacher has students signal 'thumbs up' if they agree with the student's answer, 'thumbs down' if they don't agree.

Examples: swing on the swings or slide down the slide
white milk or chocolate milk
crayons or markers
paint a picture, make something out of clay
sing a song, play a song

Additional examples may be needed to make sure students understand the concept.

The teacher reads the book *Which Would You Rather Be?*

The teacher groups students in heterogeneous pairs. The teacher selects choices from the book. (stick or stone, cat or dog, snake or crocodile, mouse or elephant, duck or fox) For each choice, partners take turns asking their partner "Which would you rather be?" The teacher tells students to stand if their partner's choice was the first item. Together, students count the total number of partners who chose the first item. The teacher tells the pairs to decide what was given up if the first choice was made. One pair is chosen to respond. Using 'thumbs up' for agree or 'thumbs down' for disagree, the other students signal whether they think the answer was correct or incorrect. This process is repeated for partners who chose the second item. Using the signal '1' or '2', each student indicates which choice had more students. The teacher uses the same process for other choices from the book.

Group Processing: Students tell their partner one thing they liked about working together.

Individual Accountability:
The teacher gives each student a response sheet. The teacher tells the students they have a choice for playing after school. They can only do one of the two things – play outside or play inside. Each student draws a picture of what they chose to do and a picture of what they gave up when their choice was made.

My choice	**What I gave up**

William Steig author information
http://us.macmillan.com/author/williamsteig

Summary

Teachers can use a variety of cooperative grouping structures to build cooperative learning lesson activities. When planning cooperative lessons, teachers need to be sure to include: the lesson objective, the materials needed, the procedure for the lesson, group processing, and individual accountability.

Cooperative learning lesson activities provide opportunities for students to practice using group roles to enhance their participation and the success of the group. The teacher can use cooperative lesson activities to have the students practice group skills. Group building activities can be created to extend the cooperative lessons.

Footnotes

[1] Katz, B. (1998). The Assembly Line. *American History Poems.* New York: Scholastic.

[2] Lyman, L., Foyle, H. C., & Azwell, T. S. (1993). Change for a Quarter. *Cooperative Learning in the Elementary Classroom.* Washington, DC: National Education Association, p. 43-44.

[3] Adapted from Lyman, L., & Foyle, H.C. (1990). Colorful Language. *Cooperative Grouping for Interactive Learning: Students, Teachers, and Administrators.* Washington, DC: National Education Association, p. 84-85.

[4] Adapted from Drake, J. (1991). Native American Dwellings of the Past. *Cooperative Learning in the Elementary Classroom* by H. C. Foyle, L. Lyman, and S. A. Thies. Washington, DC: National Education Association, p. 117-118.

[5] Adapted from Lyman & Foyle (1990), p. 67.

Chapter Eight
Promoting Active Involvement

'The class would continue on this way for the entire morning, and Klaus would feel his eyes glaze over – the phrase 'glaze over' here means 'ache slightly out of boredom.'

The Austere Academy
by Lemony Snicket
Scholastic, 2000, p. 59.
www.lemonysnicket.com

The time available for teaching and learning is a finite resource which most teachers agree is not sufficient for doing all the things they would like to do with their students. To make the most of the time available, teachers need to encourage students to be actively involved in learning and to structure activities in the classroom so that time is used as productively as possible. Dealing with student misbehavior appropriately and avoiding unnecessary distractions while teaching saves time and promotes student involvement. Effective communication with students and working with students to manage conflict helps to make the classroom a positive and need fulfilling place. Communication with parents and family members also helps to reduce misunderstandings and potentially time consuming conflicts. Checking for understanding helps the teacher to help make the most of available learning time and to reduce student frustration.

Dealing with Minor Misbehavior Efficiently

In previous chapters, the need to manage and structure the classroom so that students feel safe and so that students' needs are met was discussed. Creating a safe, need fulfilling classroom environment will help to prevent a great deal of student misbehavior. Promoting collaboration and cooperation among students also decreases the likelihood that undesirable behavior will occur in most classroom settings. Since it is not possible to prevent all student misbehavior from occurring, however, teachers need to be able to deal with minor misbehavior effectively without wasting valuable learning time.

According to Dreikurs and others, teachers can inadvertently encourage misbehavior by dealing with minor misbehavior ineffectively. When students misbehave, they usually want one of four things: attention, power, revenge, or to avoid failure. These wants, or 'mistaken goals', differ from the needs students have as identified by Glasser and others. Time is lost and frustration occurs when the teacher inadvertently reinforces what the student wanted instead of dealing with the misbehavior effectively.

Teachers can often identify the goal of a student's behavior (what the student wants) by their own reaction to the behavior. If the student is seeking inappropriate attention, which is the most common goal, the teacher will usually feel frustrated or annoyed by the student's behavior.

If a student is seeking inappropriate power, the teacher's feelings are more likely to be anger or resentment toward the student. If the student is seeking revenge, the teacher will usually feel hurt and then want to retaliate against the student. If a student is seeking to avoid failure by not putting forth effort to accomplish learning tasks, the teacher will usually feel frustrated in trying to help the student.

When the teacher responds to student behavior by providing what the student wants, the inappropriate behavior is reinforced and is more likely to continue to reoccur. For example, if a student is seeking attention and the teacher gives attention, even negatively, the student's inappropriate demands for attention will be reinforced. If a student is seeking to avoid failure by showing they have inadequate skills to complete learning tasks, the student's behavior is reinforced if the teacher gives too much help, pities, or criticizes the student.

When the teacher responds in appropriate ways to student misbehavior, the teacher can save time, energy, and frustration. For example, if the teacher ignores a student's inappropriate demand for attention by using extinction and later responds by giving the desired attention when the student is behaving appropriately, this appropriate teacher response reduces the probability that the student will continue to make inappropriate demands for attention and makes appropriate behavior more likely.[1]

The 4 Mistaken Behaviors

According to Glasser and others, when teachers continue to use strategies that are not working to correct minor misbehavior in the classroom, they are frustrating themselves and their students as well as wasting time and energy. To deal with inappropriate behavior effectively, the teacher must be willing to adapt his or her strategies. The willingness to change approaches that are not working is an important attribute of successful teachers. The teacher's ability to build a productive and positive relationship with each student is the best way to prevent a great deal of minor misbehavior and to deal with misbehavior effectively when it does occur.[2]

"Cooperative Discipline – Dreikurs and Albert"

Avoiding Unnecessary Distractions

Well-planned lessons make the best use of available time. When the teacher has the necessary supplies for the lesson ready, has thought of appropriate examples in advance, and identified connections in the lesson with what the students have learned or experienced previously, teaching can proceed efficiently. Effective teachers plan extra material for their lessons in case the lesson proceeds more quickly than expected.

Kounin identified four ways in which teachers interrupt the *smoothness and momentum* of teaching and learning: dangles, flip-flops, thrusts, and stimulus bound divergences. When teachers become aware they are interrupting the smoothness and momentum of their lessons and reduce the occurrences of these divergences, valuable time is saved and student confusion and misdirection is minimized.[3]

Dangles occur when the teacher leaves a topic or activity without finishing the activity to do something else. For example, the teacher notices that it is time to get the students lined up to go to music class. He or she instructs the students to put away the math assignment they are working on; they will come back to the assignment after music class.

Since students are usually paying the most attention to the teacher at the beginning and at the end of a learning activity, the dangle does not use the end of the activity time period effectively. By timing the lesson activity to end a few minutes before the transition to the next activity is to take place, the teacher provides time for closure at the end of the activity.

Closure provides an opportunity for the teacher to check for student understanding of the important ideas from the day's lesson. Checking for understanding lets the teacher know where he or she needs to begin teaching during the next instructional period and what reteaching may be needed. Students also have an opportunity for a quick review of the ideas that should be remembered from the lesson.

Flip-flops occur when the teacher leaves something he or she is teaching to return to a previously unfinished activity. For example, after returning from music class, the teacher begins the social studies lesson. As the lesson begins, the teacher recalls that the students did not have enough time to complete the math assignment before they left for music. The flip-flop occurs if the teacher leaves the social studies activity without completing it and returns to the math activity. As with the dangle, student confusion and misdirection can occur and time is not being used effectively.

Thrusts happen when teachers give examples or add extraneous information into a lesson which may be interesting and familiar to the teacher but which students cannot connect to the lesson or to their own experiences. Such information may be confusing to the students or may cause them to become bored or disengaged. Similar to thrusts, *stimulus bound divergences* occur when the teacher distracts the students by calling the students' attention to something completely unrelated to the lesson which is being taught. By focusing instruction on ideas specifically related to the lesson and by connecting learning to previous lessons and to student experiences, better use is made of teaching time and potential student confusion, boredom, and distraction is less likely to occur.[4]

Additional information on Kounin's ideas can be found at this website:
www.pecentral.org/climate/april99article.html

Some of the thrusts and stimulus bound divergences that occur in the classroom come from the students instead of the teacher. Many students are eager to share information and experiences that they feel are related to the topic but which serve as distractions or time wasters as teacher thrusts do. Some students want attention so badly that they insert irrelevant or humorous information into the lesson when called upon, distracting the teacher and their fellow classmates as a stimulus bound divergence by the teacher would.

Because appropriate student ideas, opinions, and feelings are important to the instructional process and student involvement in an interactive classroom, the teacher needs to be careful when limiting student contributions to the lesson. The most common and compelling reason for doing so is that there is simply not enough time to let students share as much as they would like to. Also, when too much listening is required of students, they may become bored and off task behavior can become a concern. Letting students know there may be time later to for more sharing is one way of dealing with these problems. Collaborative and cooperative activities can also let more students share ideas during a lesson.

Communicating Positively with Students

Whenever possible, teachers need to communicate with their students in positive and nurturing ways. Students are usually less involved and less productive in classrooms where communication from the teacher is neutral or negative. For example, teachers can communicate feedback about achievement and behavior, even feedback that has a negative or potentially threatening message, in a positive way. Positive communication makes it more likely that the student will listen to the teacher and respond appropriately. People First Language is one strategy for positive communication.

Some Strategies for Positive Communication

Use positive reinforcement and feedback frequently
Accept and reflect the student's feelings
Encourage the student
Make an affirmation statement about the student
Ask a question to clarify the situation

Letting students know that their appropriate work and behavior is noticed and appreciated by the teacher helps to reinforce the teacher's expectations while building trust and student self esteem. Positive reinforcement is using words and expressions such "good job", "awesome", and "way to go". Positive reinforcement lets students know that their academic and behavioral efforts are recognized and appreciated by the teacher. Teachers should vary the specific words they use to provide positive reinforcement so that the reinforcement seems heartfelt and not just routine or insincere to the students.

More useful than positive reinforcement is positive feedback. Positive feedback lets the students know that their work or behavior is appreciated, but adds information about what the student did that was noteworthy. This also helps reinforce expectations and lets the students know what they can do next time to be successful again. Positive feedback for behavior might include comments such as "thank you for raising your hand" and "great job of lining up quietly".

Positive feedback for student work include comments such as "very neat and well organized", "the pictures you drew were outstanding", or "you found more than one terrific source for your report". Positive feedback can be used to stimulate further work with comments such as "your description of the setting in your story was great – tell me more about it". Written comments on students' assignments are more meaningful to students than a grade or percentage.

To maintain a positive classroom climate, it is important for the teacher to use positive reinforcement and positive feedback more frequently than extinction or negative reinforcement. It requires practice and commitment for the teacher to notice those students who are being cooperative and helpful instead of focusing on those who are not. For example, if the class is noisy and the teacher is ready to begin, providing positive feedback to the students who are ready, "Chad and Amy are ready to go" or "Juan's table is paying attention", will usually get the students' attention as effectively as focusing on those students not cooperating.

Accepting and reflecting the feelings of a student is another way to build trust with students and to help solve problems. For example, a student may tell the teacher "I hate Aaron." The teacher could respond by telling the student that it is unacceptable to 'hate' people. In this example, the teacher did not listen and respond effectively to what the student said. While the immediate result may be that the student suppresses his or her anger, the long term effects could be detachment from the teacher and from other students, increased tension among students, or violence between students.

A more effective response to "I hate Aaron" would be to seek additional information: "Why are you angry with Aaron?" After the teacher understands the reasons for the misunderstanding with Aaron and lets the student know his or her feelings are understood, the teacher can help the student come up with a plan to deal with the problem that does not escalate the conflict.[5]

Another strategy for positive communication is to encourage the student. Students may become discouraged when learning new or difficult concepts. To encourage one or more students, the teacher might remind the students of other things that were difficult but which the students successfully accomplished. For example, the teacher notices that a student has only completed about two thirds of his assignment. The teacher could encourage the student by noticing, "You have almost all the problems done. Good job – keep going."

Affirmation statements let the students know the teacher believes in them and has confidence in their ability. For example, the teacher could say to the class, "You will be having a substitute this afternoon while I am at a meeting. I know I can count on you to behave well for her." The teacher could also use an affirmation statement to let a student know that the teacher values the student but that a behavior was inappropriate, "I know you would never have said that to him if you knew how much it would hurt his feelings."

Asking an appropriate question can be a more positive response in some instances than making a statement. For example, if a student is not doing what he is supposed to be doing, the teacher could ask, "what are you supposed to be doing now?" If a student has submitted an assignment which the teacher suspects is not her work, the teacher could ask, "Are you sure this is your work?"

Of course, it is not always appropriate to respond to student work or behavior positively. It is sometimes necessary to let a student know their work or their behavior is unacceptable. Correcting misbehavior should be done privately whenever possible to avoid humiliating or embarrassing the student. After correcting a student, it is very important for the teacher to notice any effort the student makes to improve and provide positive reinforcement or positive feedback for the effort.

Positive communication can become ineffective if students are not sure the teacher is sincere. For example, if the teacher is sarcastic with the students at times, it may cause students to question positive statements the teacher makes. Asking a rhetorical question such as "Would you like me to call your mother?" instead of making a statement "Please stop that behavior" can also confuse students and make them question the teacher's intent even when the teacher intends to be positive.

Active Listening

Active listening is one of the most important skills modeled by effective teachers. By listening actively to students, teachers let their students know that they are valued by the teacher and that their ideas are important. Teachers can also save teaching time by taking time to understand what students are saying and thinking. Active listening helps the teacher to identify potential causes of stress and anxiety in learning, to identify students' misconceptions about what they are learning, and to make connections between what is being taught and the students' interests and experiences.

According to Stephen Covey, the most effective and meaningful kind of listening is empathic listening. When teachers employ empathic listening, their goal is first to understand what the student is trying to communicate before responding. Empathic listening lets the student know that the teacher understands both the message the student is trying to communicate and the feelings the student is having. Active listening can help the teacher to communicate effectively with students, parents, and family members.

"Seek First to Understand"

It is important that the teacher's response be appropriate for the kind of message that was communicated. For example, when a student or parent's message primarily focuses on a feeling ("I don't like ...", "I'm angry about ..."), the teacher should first respond to the feeling before providing information or ideas that may solve the problem. Taking time to understand the message of a student or parent and to respond appropriately can save time and effort by building trust and preventing misunderstandings or conflicts which may be time consuming to resolve.

Websites about active listening and teaching listening skills to students:

New Horizons for Learning
www.newhorizons.org/voices/unger.htm

Active Listening for the Classroom
http://712educators.about.com/cs/activelistening/a/activelistening.htm

Listening Games and Activities
www.articlesforeducators.com/dir/language_arts/listening_skills/listening_games.asp

Raising and Lowering Student Anxiety and Concern

While some student anxiety and concern is helpful to keep students involved and on task, too much anxiety or concern can interfere with student learning. Statements made by the teacher can increase or decrease the amount of anxiety or concern that students are experiencing. Increasing student anxiety or concern can increase student attention, promote more careful work habits, encourage thinking and problem solving, and hold students accountable for what is being learned. Decreasing student anxiety or concern can reduce anxiety and tension when these factors become unproductive, help students to relax and do their best work on a task you know they are ready for, reduce frustration and worry, and encourage students to keep trying when learning becomes difficult.

In the following examples, statements that would increase or decrease anxiety and concern are contrasted. Neither group of statements is necessarily better than the other group – each kind of statement can be appropriate depending on student learning needs, attitudes, and behavior.[6]

Statements to Increase Student Anxiety or Concern	Statements to Decrease Student Anxiety or Concern
I'll be collecting your papers in five minutes.	You have plenty of time to finish.
This is a test, so be sure to check your work carefully.	These are only for practice.
This one is harder.	Here are some easier ones.
I'll be grading these papers and showing them to your parents at conference time.	You'll be the only one to see the answers you write.
You need to work more carefully. There are too many errors in your work.	You're doing just fine – relax.
Be ready to take notes – this will be on the test.	I have a handout with all the important information you need.
I'll only say these once.	I can repeat any you didn't get when we finish.

"Lowering Test Anxiety by a Middle School Teacher"

Effective Examples and Questions

Students are more likely to be actively involved in the instructional process when the teacher communicates examples and uses effective questioning strategies. Teachers need to plan their examples and questions before a lesson to make the best use of the available teaching time.[7]

Suggestions for Using Effective Examples

1. Use clear and simple examples in the early stages of learning to minimize student confusion.

2. Relate examples to previous learnings, student experiences, and student interests.

3. Teach exceptions only after a concept has been well learned. (example – a whale is a mammal)

4. Ask students to generate their own examples after a concept has been well learned

5. Avoid examples that detract from the learning (example – the cost of tickets to a football game played by teams who provoke strong emotions in the students)

Like examples, questions can enhance student learning or detract from it. One of the most important principles of effective questioning is to actively involve the students by making them feel that any student may be called upon to answer. Every pupil response strategies (explained later in this chapter) are examples of effective ways to involve all students in responding to questions.

Asking Effective Questions

1. With new or unfamiliar learning, ask simple, direct questions.

2. As students become more familiar with a topic or concept, ask open-ended questions to help students apply and analyze information.

3. When asking for an individual student response, allow appropriate wait time (a minimum of 15 seconds between the question and calling on a student) to encourage more students to respond. Don't encourage students to shout out answers.

4. Listen to student responses for clues about how well they are understanding.

5. Use mistakes to extend student learning. ("That would be correct if we were talking about …")

6. Ask students for clarification. ("Why did you say that?" "What were you thinking about?")

7. Avoid questions that call for rhetorical responses.

8. Involve as many students as possible in responding to questions.

Class Meetings

Class meetings have many advantages in the classroom. Regular class meetings can promote student responsibility and caring. Some of the purposes for which class meetings can be used are:

Ways to Use Class Meetings

students share good news about other students
group processing – how well are we working together as a class?
discussion of rules and procedures that may need updating
summary at the end of a project or learning activity
problem solving
teacher and students plan for an upcoming event such as a field trip

---

Teachers need to make sure their expectations for class meetings are appropriate for the developmental levels and characteristics of the students. Class meetings will not work well if sufficient trust has not been built in the classroom.

To make class meetings work successfully, teachers need to model procedures for speaking, for disagreeing constructively, and for reaching agreement. It may be helpful to develop a list of guidelines for class meetings with the students and update the list as needed.[8]

In order to be effective, class meetings need to be held on a regular basis. A time limit can be set in order to keep students on task. At the end of a class meeting, the teacher can have one or two students summarize what was discussed at the meeting or summarize the meeting him or herself.

Website Twenty Kinds of Class Meetings
www.ethicsed.org/consulting/meetingideas.htm

"Class Meeting About Being Respectful"

Communication with Parents and Family Members

Communicating with parents and family members can be time consuming and sometimes frustrating. Because teachers and family members are busy, appropriate communication can make the best use of times available for communicating, such as parent and teacher conferences, and avoid time consuming misunderstandings that can erode trust.

At the beginning of the school year, the following information may be useful to parents and family members.

What is the mission statement of the school?

What is the teacher's philosophy of teaching?
How long has the teacher been teaching? Other professional information?
How can I contact the teacher if I have a question or concern?
What are the rules of the school and rules of the classroom?
What will my child be studying this year?
How much homework can I expect my child to have this year?
How can I help my child at home?
What supplies will my child need to bring to school?
What other things can my child bring to school?
What clothing or items are not acceptable at school?
Arrival and departure times?
Daily schedule?
Other adults in the classroom (student teachers, paraeducators, volunteers)?
Other teachers my child will work with (music, art, p. e., media specialist)?
Grading policies?
When will graded work be sent home?

Example of a First of the Year Newsletter to Family Members, Page One

Example of a First of the Year Newsletter to Family Members, Page two

Example of a Calendar for Students and Family Members

Example of Suggestions for Parents and Family Members

> **Suggestions for Written Communications from the Teacher to Family Members**
>
> Be sure that written communication is the appropriate medium to use.
> Be sure that you are addressing the parent, guardian or other family member correctly (name and preferred title).
> Always have someone proofread what you send home.
> The tone of any written communication needs to be positive and professional.
> Be sensitive to gender.
> Avoid jargon or other words that may be unfamiliar to the reader
> Keep a copy of anything you send home.

Some teachers find it useful to phone family members of the students in the class at the beginning of the school year to make a proactive contact. This is helpful if the teacher needs to call later with a problem or concern.

Experience has made some family members believe that any contact from the school is because of a problem with the student. One teacher decided to make sure she made at least one positive contact with every family each month. With the assistance of the Parent Teacher Organization at her school, she purchased post cards from the Post Office. During the month, as she saw something positive or creative from a student, she took a moment to write a brief note to the family and mailed the post card. At the end of the month, the teacher observed the children for whom a post card had not been sent yet to find something positive they were doing. Family members loved the positive contacts.

As a kindergarten teacher, Sheila Broyles has a particularly creative way of getting to know the families of her students.

"Home Visits and Bedtime Stories"

Conferences with Parents and Family Members

Conferences with parents and family members provide valuable opportunities to learn more about the student and to work cooperatively with family members. When teachers encourage family members to share during the conference, they can find out useful information about the student:

What Family Members Can Bring to the Conference

How the family member feels about school, concerns, questions

How the student feels about school, what they say about what they are learning and doing in school

Ways the child learns best

Interests, skills, talents that the child displays outside of school, outside activities the child is involved in

Unusual or stressful conditions in the home that might affect the child's attitude or performance in school

Previous experiences in school

Responsibilities, chores, expectations for the child outside of school

---

Example of a Newsletter with Suggestions for Conferences, page one

Example of a Newsletter with Suggestions for Conferences, page two

Suggestions for Effective Conferences with Family Members

The teacher's goal for every conference – The family members will leave the conference feeling more positive about the school and about the child.

Analyze – As with a lesson to be planned and taught, the teacher must consider the information available about the student and select the most important and useful information to be shared during the conference time. Identify one or more questions to encourage the family member to share information as well.

Listening – The teacher needs to listen actively to information and ideas the family member may be sharing and respond positively to questions asked.

Positive tone – Conferences need to begin and end on a positive tone. If some of the information shared during the conference is unpleasant, the teacher needs to return the conference to a positive tone at the end by summarizing the positive attributes of the student and what the family member and the teacher can do to support the student.

Examples – Positive and negative comments to family members need to be supported by specific examples. A portfolio of student work samples is useful.

Closure – End by agreeing on the next step – for example, a future conference to check progress, having a family member work with the child on homework, following up with the nurse if a health concern is identified.

Reflection – After the conference, the teacher should reflect on the conference, making notes about new information learned and agreements made with the family members.

It is inevitable that teachers will sometimes deal with parents and family members who are upset or angry. When confronted by a family member with a concern or complaint, the teacher should first thank the family member for bringing the concern to the teacher. Most teachers would prefer to have an opportunity to address a concern or complaint themselves and not have a family member go "over their heads" to the principal, the superintendent, or a school board member.

When dealing with an upset family member, active listening is especially important. The teacher needs to identify both the feeling the family member has and the information that he or she is bringing to the teacher. When the teacher is sure that he or she understands the concern or complaint, it is often useful to ask, "what can I do to help?" Sometimes, the teacher's courteous response and active listening have defused the anger and the family member doesn't want anything done; he or she appreciates being listened to with respect.

After discussing a complaint or concern, it is important to end with a mutual understanding of what the next step will be, if any. Teachers should not agree to take responsibilities which are unreasonable or unworkable, for example, writing a note home to the parent each day. Teachers and family members can always agree on one thing – they want what is best for the child involved.

When a family member comes with a concern or complaint, the teacher should always inform the administrator or designee so he or she is aware of the problem in case the family member contacts the administrator, superintendent, or a school board member. Administrators appreciate teachers who keep them informed of what is going on.

Websites for communication with parents and family members:

Teacher-Parent Collaboration
www.teachervision.fen.com/education-and-parents/resource/3730.html

Communicating with Parents
http://ceep.crc.uiuc.edu/eecearchive/digests/2003/mendoza03.html

Communicating with Parents During Sensitive or Difficult Situations
http://illinoisearlylearning.org/chat/stephens/sup.htm

Checking for Student Understanding

A crucial component of effective teaching is overtly and consistently checking to assess the students' understanding of what is being taught. For example, the teacher needs to identify parts of a lesson which may be confusing to some or all of the students, to determine whether the students understand the directions for assignments and activities, and to decide on the next steps in the instructional process based on data from students. Appropriately checking student understanding can save time and reduce student frustration.

A strategy for checking student understanding that is usually ineffective is to ask the students if there are any questions. Students who have questions may be reluctant to ask a question because they do not want to appear stupid. Even if the teacher has built sufficient trust with the so that the students feel comfortable in asking questions, some students may think they understand the information adequately even when they do not. Some students may be so confused that they cannot form an articulate question. Finally, some students may not be paying attention.

Two more effective ways to check for student understanding during a lesson are to provide wait time during instruction and to use strategies which require every student to respond to questions designed to check their comprehension. Wait time involves imposing a short waiting period of 15-20 seconds after a question is asked of the students. During wait time, students do not raise their hands, talk, or blurt out answers. The use of wait time allows students time for thinking instead of competing to see which student can respond quickest. This strategy is used in the cooperative strategy *Think-Pair-Share* which is described in the cooperation and collaboration chapter.

When wait time is not used, most teachers have experienced responses from students overly eager to get attention by answering a question with a response that is incorrect or unrelated to the question. Such responses take valuable instructional time and are often distracting to the teacher and to the other students in the class. Enforcing a hands-down wait time before accepting responses to questions will usually encourage more students to share ideas and increase on task responses.

Using strategies which require an observable response from every student, sometimes called Every Pupil Response (EPR) strategies, can provide more accurate information to the teacher about students' understanding of the lesson and will involve students more actively in the lesson.

> **Examples of Every Pupil Response (EPR) Strategies**
>
> thumbs up if you understand, thumb to the side if you understand a little, thumbs down if you don't understand
>
> thumbs up if you agree with the answer, thumbs down if you don't agree
>
> index card with a red circle for disagree, green circle on the back for agree
>
> given examples by the teacher, show the correct response by holding up 1, 2, 3, or 4 fingers
>
> individual marker boards or slates for recording the answer, hold up the board for teacher checking
>
> electronic clickers
>
> choral response from the group (not accurate for checking individual student understanding)

An additional EPR checking strategy is the 'windows' strategy. Have each student fold a sheet of letter size paper in fourths. When the teacher asks a question or gives the students a problem to solve, each student writes their answer on one of the 'window panes' (one of the fourths) and holds it up to provide feedback to the teacher. At the conclusion of the lesson, the sheets can be collected by the teacher to encourage active participation and accountability.

Maintaining the students' attention during the lesson is easier when wait time and EPR strategies are used. When students to tend to lose focus during instruction, the following suggestions can be used:

Suggestions for Getting Students Focused
Jennifer Anderson

When teaching, everyone must be focused:

- all student chairs turned toward you
- ask questions to involve the students in each step
- if possible, ask every student a question or use every pupil response strategy

When students are not focused (not participating, playing around, talking):

- first, try to figure out why
- second, involve the students when presenting ideas and information
- third, have everyone stand up and stretch and make sure all distractions have been removed (toys, books, erasers, etc.)
- fourth, change the way the students are completing the activity (example: take paper and pencil away and only use white boards)

Other checking for understanding strategies can be found at the following websites:

Pre-Assessment
http://daretodifferentiate.wikispaces.com/Pre-Assessment

Every Pupil Response Cards
www.proteacher.net/discussions/showthread.php?p=685730

Summary

Making effective use of the time available for teaching and learning is a top priority for successful teachers. Teachers can use effective strategies for dealing efficiently with student misbehavior, for maintaining momentum and smoothness while teaching, and for checking for student understanding. These strategies help the teacher utilize time appropriately while reducing off task behavior from students and promoting their active involvement.

Effective communication, including active listening, is necessary for teachers to work effectively and efficiently with students and with their parents and family members. Communication strategies can improve relationships and reduce misunderstandings. Both oral and written communication should be grammatically and conventionally accurate, professional, and tactful.

Active student involvement is also encouraged by helping students acquire skills to manage conflicts which inevitably occur in classrooms. Classroom meetings can be effective ways to promote student involvement and solve problems.

Additional Resources

Albert, L. (2003). *Cooperative discipline: Teacher's handbook.* Circle Pines, MN: American Guidance Service.

Bianco, A. (2002). *One-Minute discipline: Classroom management strategies that work!* San Francisco: Jossey-Bass.

Blackburn, B. (2005). *Classroom motivation from a to z.* Larchmont, NY: Eye on Education.

Brookhart, S. M. (2008). *How to give effective feedback to your students.* Alexandria, VA: Association for Supervision and Curriculum Development.

Coloroso, B. (2009). *The bully, the bullied, and the bystander.* New York, NY: Harper.

Dahlstrom, L. M. (1994). *Doing the days: A year's worth of creative journaling, drawing, listening, reading, thinking, arts & crafts activities for children ages 8-12.* Minneapolis: Free Spirit Publishing.

Davis, C., & Yang, A. (2005). *Parents and teachers working together.* Turners Falls, MA: Northeast Foundation for Children.

Dodge, J. (2009). *25 quick formative assessments for a differentiated classroom.* New York, NY: Scholastic.

Drew, N. (2004). *Kids guide to working out conflicts: How to keep cool, stay safe, and get along.* Minneapolis, MN: Free Spirit Publishing.

Dyches, T. T., Carter, N. J., & Prater, M. A. (2012). *A teacher's guide to communicating with parents: Practical strategies for developing successful relationships.* Upper Saddle River, NJ: Pearson.

Fisher, D., & Frey N. (2007). *Checking for understanding: Formative assessment techniques for your classroom.* Alexandria, VA: Association for Supervision and Curriculum Development.

Gestwicki, C. (2010). *Home, school, and community relations* (7th ed.). Belmont, CA: Wadsworth.

Lee, E., Menkart, D., & Okazawa-Rey, M. (2004). *Beyond heroes and holidays: A practical guide to k-12 anti-racist, multicultural education and staff development.* Milwaukee, WI: Rethinking Schools.

McElherne, M. L., & Vinton, K. (2006). *Quick and lively classroom activities: Meaningful ways to keep kids engaged during transition time, downtime, or anytime.* Minneapolis: Free Spirit Publishing.

McEwan, E. K. (2005). *How to deal with parents who are angry, troubled, afraid, or just plain crazy.* Thousand Oaks, CA: Corwin.

Payne, R. K. (2006). *Working with parents: Building relationships for student success.* Highlands, TX: aha! Process, Inc.

Roser, S. L. (2009). *Energizers! 88 quick movement activities that refresh and refocus, k-6.* Turners Falls, MA: Northeast Foundation for Children.

Silberg, J., Schiller, P., Berry, M., & Oshiver, M. (2002). *The complete book and cc set of rhymes, songs, poems, fingerplays, and chants.* Beltsville, MD: Gryphon House.

Springer, S., Alexander, B., & Persiani-Becker, K. (2006). *The creative teacher: An encyclopedia of ideas to energize your curriculum.* New York, NY: McGraw-Hill.

Thompson, B. (1999). *Take five minutes: 365 calendar-related editing activities.* Westminster, CA: Teacher Created Materials.

Thurston, C.M. (2003). *Surviving last period on Fridays and other desperate situations.* Fort Collins, CO: Cottonwood Press.

Wilson, C. C. (2010). *Perfect phrases for classroom teachers: Hundreds of ready-to-use phrases for parent-teacher conferences, report cards, IEPs, and other school documents.* New York, NY: McGraw-Hill.

Footnotes

[1] Larrivee, B. (2009). *Authentic Classroom Management: Creating a Learning Community and Building Reflective Practice* (3rd ed.). Upper Saddle River, NJ: Merrill, p. 170-176.

[2] Glasser, W. (1998). *Choice Theory: A New Psychology of Personal Freedom.* New York, NY: Harper, p. 19-24.

[3] Kounin, J. (1977). *Discipline and Group Management in the Classroom.* New York, NY: Holt, Rinehart, and Winston.

[4] Evertson, C. M., & Emmer, E. T. (2009). *Classroom Management for Elementary Teachers.* 8th edition. Upper Saddle River, NJ: Merrill, p. 108-112.

[5] Covey, S. R. (1989). *The Seven Habits of Highly Effective People.* New York, NY: Simon and Schuster, p. 239-255.

[6] Adapted from Lyman, L., Wilson, A. P, Garhart, C. K, Heim, M. O., & Winn, W. O. (1987).
Clinical Instruction and Supervision for Accountability (2nd ed.). Dubuque, IA: Kendall/Hunt, p. 62-63.

[7] Lyman et. al, pages 52 and 53.

[8] Lyman, Foyle, & Azwell, p. 51-52.

Chapter Nine
Activities to Use Class Time Productively

'When they began to count all the time that was available, what with 60 seconds in a minute and 60 minutes in an hour and 24 hours in a day and 365 days in a year, it seemed as if there was much more of it than could ever be used. ... People wasted it and even gave it away.'

Tock the Watchdog
in *The Phantom Tollbooth*
Norton Juster, Random House, 2005, p. 34

According to Madeline Hunter (2004), sponge activities are "learning activities that soak up precious time that would otherwise be lost."[1] Sponge activities can provide opportunities for group building activities, for critical and creative thinking, and for practicing skills. At the beginning of class, for example, sponge activities can be used to focus student attention on the learning activity, to review a concept or idea, or to practice a skill needed for the activity which will be taking place. Think Pair Share, a cooperative learning strategy developed by Frank Lyman, Jr., works well with many sponge activities.[2] The Think Pair Share strategy is described in Chapter 6.

Purposes for Sponge Activities

Something productive for students do while waiting for class to begin

Something for students who finish an activity early to do

Help make more productive use of transition time

Fill unexpected blocks of time

Change of pace during a lesson

Opportunities to practice and extend academic and social skills

Opportunities for group building (see Chapter 4)

Opportunities to practice critical and creative thinking and problem solving

Activities to include in a kit for a substitute teacher in case of teacher absence

Where to Locate Ideas for Sponge Activities

Teachers' editions of student textbooks often contain a number of ideas for integrating and extending concepts being taught. While there is not enough time to use all of these ideas, some of the ideas that promote student interest, encourage cooperation, or provide opportunities for critical and creative thinking can be good sources for sponge activities.

The Internet can provide many web sites for teachers to use for sponge activities. Activities can be used for remediation, practice, enrichment, or to extend concepts that are being taught by the teacher. Some suggested web sites for sponge activities follow.

Selected Websites for Sponge Activities

Education Place – Houghton Mifflin
www.eduplace.com/activity/

Education World
www.educationworld.com/a_lesson/lesson168.shtml

Fact Monster
www.factmonster.com

Games for Groups
www.gamesforgroups.com/teambuildinggames.html

Great Web Sites for Kids
http://www.ala.org/gwstemplate.cfm?section=greatwebsites&template=/cfapps/gws/default.cfm

Idaho Teachers
www.foridahoteachers.org/anchor_activities.htm

Imagination Factory – Kids at Art
www.kid-at-art.com

Internet TESL Journal
http://iteslj.org/games/

Kansas Wildlife and Parks
www.kdwp.state.ks.us/news/Other-Services/Education/Wildlife-Education-Services/Wildlife-Education-Materials

Kid Activities
www.kidactivities.net/?tag=/sponge+activities

Library of Congress
www.loc.gov/teachers/

Online Education
www.onlinecollegeguru.com/blog/education/100-sponge-activities-2/

Reading is Fundamental
www.rif.org/kids/readingplanet.htm

San Francisco Museum of Science
www.exploratorium.edu/explore/

Smarty Games
www.smartygames.com

Thinkfinity-Verizon Foundation
www.thinkfinity.org/in-the-classroom

U.S. Geological Survey
http://education.usgs.gov/

Yak's Corner – Detroit News in Education
www.nieonline.com/detroit/index.cfm

Examples of Sponge Activities

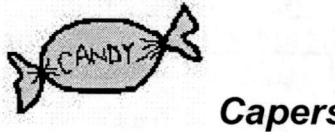

Capers

Use the clues to identify the name of a candy.

people who help drowning swimmers	her baseball team plays Charlie Brown's team
a happy farmer	one tenth of a million dollars
the fourth planet from the sun	what every worker looks forward to
people who often drop things	the noise cellophane makes when crumpled
laughs quietly	"All for one and one for all!"
the galaxy in which we live	a highway covered with stones
what a bee gets from a very small flower	small hills on which baseball pitchers stand

Bonus – *These are harder.*
  bread for a movie character played by Dustin Hoffman
  what a teenage girl might call a large, attractive boy
  a female infant

Answers – Candy Capers

Lifesavers	Peppermint Patty
Jolly Rancher	$100,000 bar
Mars bar	Pay Day
Butterfinger	Krackel
Snickers	Three Musketeers
Milky Way	Rocky Road
Bit o' Honey	Mounds

Bonus answers:
  Tootsie Roll
  Big Hunk
  Baby Ruth

Extending the activity – Additional candy related ideas can be found at these websites:

A Dozen Candy Ideas
www.educationworld.com/a_lesson/lesson/lesson142.shtml

Candy math
www.nea.org/tools/lessons/Candy-Colors--Figuring-the-Mean--Median--and-Mode.html

---

Ten Books about Candy

Dahl, R. (1964). *Charlie and the Chocolate Factory.* Knopf.

McGrath, B. B. (1998). *More m & m's Math.* Charlesbridge.

Marsh, C. (2007). *Mystery in Chocolate Town: Hershey, Pennsylvania.* Gallopede.

Mattern, J. (2011). *Milton Hershey: Hershey's Chocolate Creator.* Checkerboard Books.

Pallotta, J., & Bolster, R. C. (2001). *Hershey's Kisses Addition Book.* Scholastic.

Pallotta, J., & Bolster, R. C. (2003). *Hershey's Milk Chocolate Weights and Measures.* Carthwheel.

Pallotta, J., & Bolster, R. C. (2000). *Reese's Pieces Count By Fives.* Cartwheel.

Pallotta, J., & Bolster, R. C. (2002). *Twizzler's Shapes and Patterns.* Cartwheel.

Swain, R. F., & O'Brien, J. (2003). *How Sweet It Is (and Was): The History of Candy.* Holiday House.

Tunnell, M. O. (2010). *Candy Bomber: The Story of the Berlin Airlift's "Chocolate Pilot".* Charlesbridge.

Category Challenge

The teacher chooses a letter and students work together to think of responses that fit the category. Another use of the challenges is to have students use appropriate research materials in teams to locate possible responses.

Occupations or jobs that begin with an A
Foods that begin with a B
Animals that begin with a C
Cartoon characters that begin with a D
Numbers less than 100 that begin with an E
Words on a calendar that begin with F
Plants or flowers that begin with G
Parts of the body that begin with H
States that begin with I
Things to wear that begin with a J
Units of measure that begin with a K
Occupations or jobs that begin with an L
Words about time that begin with M
Community helpers that begin with N
Foods that end with O
Birds that begin with P
Companies or products that begin with Q
Professional sports teams that begin with R
Things kids try to avoid that start with S
Musical instruments that begin with T
Companies that deliver that begin with U
Things that are good for you that start with a V
Mammals that begin with W
Things you can read that contain the letter X
Sounds or noises that begin with Y
Countries of the world that contain the letter Z

Answers – Category Challenge

Other correct answers are possible.

- A accountant, astronaut, actor, actress, acrobat, artist, archaeologist, animal trainer
- B beans, bagel, bread, butter, broccoli, bacon, burrito
- C cat, chimpanzee, chipmunk, collie, Chihuahua, Cocker Spaniel, Chow
- D Daffy Duck, Donald Duck, Daisy Duck, Darkwing Duck, Donatello (teenage turtle)
- E even, eight, eighteen, eighty-one (through) eighty-nine
- F Friday, February, full moon, Father's Day, fall
- G gardenia, geranium, gladiola, grape, grass, giant sequoia
- H hair, hands, head, heart, heel, hips
- I Idaho, Illinois, Indiana, Iowa
- J jacket, jammies, jersey, jeans, jewelry, jumper
- K karat, kilogram, kilometer, knot
- L lawyer, letter carrier, librarian, lighthouse keeper, locksmith, loan officer
- M minute, month, Monday, March, May, moment
- N nanny, neighbor, newspaper carrier, nurse, notary public, night watchman
- O potato, tomato, taco, burrito, jello
- P penguin, peregrine falcon, pheasant, pigeon, parrot, puffin, parakeet
- Q Qantas, Quaker Oats, Quaker State, Quik Trip, Q-Tip
- R Rams, Rangers, Raiders, Reds, Red Sox, Royals, Rockies
- S school work, shadows, shots, spankings, spinach, strangers
- T tambourine, tenor saxophone, timpani, triangle, trumpet, tuba
- U U. S. Postal Service, United Parcel, United Airlines, U. S. Air, Union Pacific Railroad
- V vacation, vaccinations, vegetables, vitamins, ventilation, vigorous exercise
- W walrus, warthog, weasel, whale, wildebeest, wolf, wolverine, woodchuck
- X x-ray, exam, textbook, example, tax form, excuse, excerpt, exhibit
- Y yap, yack, yawn, yell, yowl, yawp
- Z Zaire, Zambia, Zimbabwe, Venezuela, Brazil, Czechoslovakia, Belize

Extending the activity – Have students suggest ideas for other categories.

Other word puzzles can be found at this website:
www.funbrain.com/words.html

Cats and Dogs

Name the fictional cat or dog.

1. this cat loves lasagna and lives with Jon and Odie
2. this cat chases Tweety Bird
3. this dog from Kansas visited Oz with Dorothy
4. this dog encourages kids to "take a bite out of crime"
5. this cat is a friend of Thing One and Thing Two
6. this cat lives next door to Charlie Brown's dog
7. Alice met this cat in Wonderland
8. this collie dog belonged to Timmy
9. Hermione Granger's cat
10. Hagrid's dog
11. Charlie Brown's dog
12. George Jetson's dog
13. Bart Simpson's dog
14. Mickey Mouse's dog
15. the Brady Bunch's dog

Extending the activity – Before sharing the answers, the teacher may want to have the students take their lists home to have family members help. Students may suggest other cats and dogs that could be added to the list.

Answers – Cats and Dogs

1. Garfield
2. Sylvester
3. Toto
4. McGruff
5. Cat in the Hat
6. World War II
7. Cheshire Cat
8. Lassie
9. Crookshanks
10. Fang
11. Snoopy
12. Astro
13. Santa's Little Helper
14. Pluto
15. Tiger

Fun pet facts and information can be found at the website:

American Veterinary Medicine Association
www.avma.org/careforanimals

Sponge Activity – Dogs

Students will discuss the meaning of these dog sayings in groups assigned by the teacher.

1. dog tired
2. going to the dogs
3. that dog won't hunt
4. hang dog expression
5. puppy love
6. (she kept) hounding him
7. dog days of summer
8. underdog
9. dog tag
10. doggie bag
11. dog-eared
12. (to be in the) doghouse

Answers – Dogs

The meanings may change in different regions or with different age groups.

1. tired, exhausted
2. hanging out with bad friends, declining performance
3. that won't work
4. looking sad or depressed
5. love between young people not thought to be serious
6. nagging or bothering
7. the hottest days of the year, usually in late July or August
8. has fewer resources, not expected to win
9. identification tag worn by members of the military
10. leftovers taken home from a restaurant or party
11. page that has one or more corners bent or folded
12. in trouble

Extending the activity – Students think of other animal related sayings.

Ten Books about Dogs

Bridwell, N. (2010, Reprint edition). *Clifford the Big Red Dog.* Scholastic.

Crisp, M., & Kelley, T. (2000). *My Dog, Cat.* Scholastic.

Erickson, J. R., & Holmes, G. L. (1998). *Hank the Cowdog: Every Dog Has His Day*. Puffin.

Franco, B., & Wertz, M. (2011). *A Dazzling Display of Dogs: Concrete Poems.* Tricycle Press.

Jennings, P. (1998). *Faith and the Electric Dogs.* Scholastic.

Kellogg, S. (1979). *Pinkerton, Behave!* Puffin.

Murphy, F., & Walz, R. (2002). *George Washington and the General's Dog.* Random House.

Rylant, C., & Howard, A. (2007). *Gooseberry Park.* Sandpiper.

Teague, M. (2002). *Dear Mrs. LaRue: Letters from Obedience School.* Scholastic.

Willems, M., & Muth, J. J. (2010). *City Dog, Country Frog.* Hyperion.

Yates, L. (2010). *Dog Loves Books.* Knopf.

Websites about fictional dogs:

Clifford the Big Red Dog
www.scholastic.com/clifford/

Hank the Cowdog
www.hankthecowdog.com

Sponge Activity – Geography Find[3]

Write the names of a city, a state, a body of water, or a country that begins with the letter at the top of the column.

	S	T	A	R
City				
States Provinces				
Body of Water				
Country				

Geography Find Answers

Other answers may be possible.

Cities
San Francisco, CA
Seattle, WA
Sydney, Australia
Taipei, Taiwan
Topeka, KS
Tokyo, Japan
Atlanta, GA
Athens, Greece
Augusta, ME
Raleigh, NC
Reykjavik, Iceland
Rome, Italy

States and Provinces
Saskatchewan
South Carolina
Tennessee
Texas
Alaska
Alberta
Arizona
Rhode Island

Bodies of Water
Salton Sea
Lake Superior
Snake River
Lake Tanganyika
Thames River
Tigris River
Aegean Sea
Amazon River
Arkansas River
Red Sea
Rhine River
Rio Grande River

Countries
Saudi Arabia
Spain
Switzerland
Taiwan
Thailand
Tunisia
Afghanistan
Angola
Australia
Romania
Russia
Rwanda

Ideas for geography lessons and activities can be found at the National Geographic website:

http://www.nationalgeographic.com/xpeditions/

How Many?

Put these in order from the smallest to the largest.

_____ the Seven Dwarfs + Snow White + the Prince
_____ value of the coin Abraham Lincoln is on
_____ number of things in a dozen
_____ number of wheels on two cars
_____ number of things in a pair
_____ number of kids in the Brady Bunch
_____ days in one week
_____ one hour before noon
_____ number of Teenage Ninja Mutant Turtles
_____ number of pins in bowling
_____ number of toes on one foot
_____ strikes a batter gets in baseball

Answers – How Many?

1. value of the coin Abraham Lincoln is on
2. number of things in a pair
3. strikes a batter gets in baseball
4. number of Teenage Ninja Mutant Turtles
5. number of toes on one foot
6. number of kids in the Brady Bunch
7. days in one week
8. number of wheels on two cars
9. the Seven Dwarfs + Snow White + the Prince
10. number of pins in bowling
11. one hour before noon
12. number of things in a dozen

Extending the activity – Have groups suggest number items to be used in a new puzzle.

Additional math games and activities can be found at this website:

Cool Math for Kids
http://coolmath4kids.com

Lucky and Unlucky

Fill in the missing words.

LUCKY	UNLUCKY
_____shoe	a black _____
_____clover	breaking a _____
_____foot	Friday the _____
see a _____, pick it up	opening an _____ inside
knock on _____	spilling _____
an _____ a day keeps the doctor away	stepping on a _____

Answers – Lucky and Unlucky

horseshoe	a black cat
four leaf clover	breaking a mirror
rabbit's foot	Friday the 13th
see a pin (penny), pick it up	opening an umbrella inside
knock on wood	spilling salt
an apple a day keeps the doctor away	stepping on a crack

Extending the activity - Have students identify other superstitions.

**Information about superstitions can be found at this Think Quest website:
http://library.thinkquest.org/5877**

National Names

Fill in the name of a country or nationality of the world to complete the items.

Example: _____ Setter = Irish setter

_____	meatballs	_____	geese
_____	shorts	_____	waffle
_____	nut	_____	ink
_____	checkers	_____	hat
_____	man-of-war	_____	treat
_____	toast	_____	sausage
_____	muffin	_____	cheese
_____	beetle	_____	goulash
_____	tape	_____	shepherd

Answers – National Names

Other answers may be possible.

Swedish meatballs, Canada geese, Bermuda shorts, Belgian waffle, Brazil nut, India ink, Chinese checkers, Panama hat, Portuguese man-of-war, Dutch treat, French toast, Polish sausage, English muffin, Swiss cheese, Japanese beetle, Hungarian goulash, Scotch tape, German shepherd

Extending the activity – Have students label the locations on a world map.

Red, White, and Blue

RED	WHITE	BLUE
the red planet	large white mammal threatened by global warming	this largest mammal can weigh 200 tons
group that helps victims of war and weather	1600 Pennsylvania Avenue	states that usually vote Democratic on election day
seafood restaurant	hamburger restaurant	specially priced meal that can change daily
she met a wolf on the way to visit her grandmother	ate a poisoned apple	Paul Bunyan's blue ox
famous reindeer	Alice followed this animal with a watch down a hole	preschool show starring a friendly dog
Boston's American League baseball team	Chicago's American League baseball team	Toronto's American League baseball team

Answers – Red, White, and Blue

Mars	polar bear	blue whale
Red Cross	the White House	blue states
Red Lobster	White Castle	blue plate special
Little Red Riding Hood	Snow White	Babe, the Blue Ox
Rudolph	the white rabbit	Blue's Clues
Boston Red Sox	Chicago White Sox	Toronto Blue Jays

Extending the activity – Have students suggest items for different colors.

Ten Books about Colors

Johnson, C. (1998). *Harold and the Purple Crayon.* 50th Anniversary Edition. HarperCollins

Katz, K. (2007). *The Colors of Us.* Henry Holt.

Khan, R., & Blackall, S. (2010). *Big Red Lollipop.* Viking.

Kissinger, K., & Krutein, W. (2002). *All the Colors That We Are: The Story of How We Get Our Skin Color.* Redleaf Press.

Liao, J. (2006). *Sound of Colors.* Little, Brown.

Lionni, L. (2006). *A Color of His Own.* Knopf.

Martin, B., Jr., & Carle, E. (2008). *Brown Bear, Brown Bear, What Do You Hear?* 40th Anniversary Edition. Henry Holt.

Sidman, J., & Zargarenski, P. (2009). *Red Sings from the Treetops: A Year in Colors.* Houghton Mifflin.

Thong, R., & Lin, G. (2001). *Red is a Dragon: A Book of Colors.* Chronicle Books.

Yolen, J., & Stemple, J. (2003). *Color Me a Rhyme: Nature Poems for Young People.* Boyds Mill Press.

TWO LETTERS

Write the two letters that sound like each word below.

Example = master of ceremonies, like a quiz show host, would be emcee or 'mc'

Description	First Letter	Second Letter
when something doesn't have anything in it		
a paper you write for school		
what happens to your teeth if you don't brush them		
some Native Americans used to live in these		
small, scary little eyes		
you might call an adorable little child this		
to be jealous of what someone else has		
what the roads and sidewalks sometimes are in the winter		
a plant that grows on old buildings, like colleges		
this one is very simple, not hard at all		
the cow that advertises Borden's dairy products		
boy on the old Andy Griffith show		

Answers – Two Letters

empty (mt)	essay (sa)	decay (dk)	tee pee (tp)
beady (bd)	cutie (qt)	envy (nv)	icy (ic)
ivy (iv)	easy (ez)	Elsie (lc)	Opie (op)

Extending the activity – Have students come up with additional examples.

What's for Lunch?[4]

Below are ingredients from food labels. Can you name the foods?

1. Cultured pasteurized grade A milk, skim milk, strawberries, sugar, corn sweeteners, nonfat milk solids, pectin, natural flavors, and lemon juice

2. Beef stock, tomatoes, potatoes, carrots, peas, green beans, corn, high fructose corn syrup, enriched alphabet macaroni, onions, celery, salt, potato starch, vegetable oil, yeast extract and hydrolyzed vegetable protein, monosodium glutamate, beef fat, dehydrated garlic, caramel color, natural flavoring, and oleoresin paprika

3. Meat by-products, water sufficient for processing horsemeat, beef by-products, poultry by-products, soy flour, salt, potassium chloride, guar gum, methionine hydroxy analogue calcium, DL-Alpha tocopheryl acetate (source of vitamin E), citric acid and ethoxyquin (preservatives), magnesium oxide, choline chloride, sodium nitrate (to promote color retention), iron carbonate, copper oxide, cobalt carbonate, vitamin A palmitate (stability improved), manganous oxide, zinc oxide, ethylenediamine dihydroiodide, thiamine mononitrate, D-activated animal sterol (source of vitamin D-3), and vitamin B-12 supplement

4. Beef, water, dextrose, salt, corn syrup, spice, sodium erythorbate, flavorings, sodium nitrate, and oleoresin of paprika

5. Red ripe tomatoes, distilled vinegar, corn syrup, salt, onion powder, spice, natural flavoring

6. Enriched wheat flour, malted barley four, potassium bromate, sugar, eggs, vegetable shortening, salt, artificial vanilla flavoring, lecithin, baking soda, and a small piece of paper

7. Sugar, milk, cocoa butter, chocolate, soya lecithin (an emulsifier), and vanillin (an artificial flavoring)

8. Tomato juice from concentrate (water, tomato concentrate), reconstituted juices of carrots, celery, beets, parsley, lettuce, watercress, spinach, with salt, vitamin C (ascorbic acid), natural flavoring, and citric acid.

Answers – What's for Lunch?

1. strawberry yogurt
2. vegetable beef soup
3. dog food
4. beef hot dog
5. tomato ketchup
6. fortune cookie
7. chocolate candy bar
8. vegetable juice

Extending the activity: Using food labels brought from home, students try to figure out the foods from the ingredients on the label.

Information about nutrition labels for kids can be found at this website:

Kids' Health
http://kidshealth.org/kid/stay_healthy/food/labels.html

Sponge Activity – ZIP Codes

Find four state ZIP Code abbreviations in each of these words or phrases.

A list of U. S. Postal Service state abbreviations
can be found at this website:
www.usps.com/ncsc/lookups/usps_abbreviations.html

---

avalanche

flaky

cartridge

utilitarian

wind chill

Mohican

Misdemeanor

compact disc

new hymnbooks

warm gaze

Answers – ZIP Codes

avalanche	va = Virginia nc = North Carolina	al = Alabama	la = Louisiana
flaky	fl = Florida ky = Kentucky	la = Louisiana	ak = Alaska
cartridge	ca = California id = Idaho	ar = Arkansas	ri = Rhode Island
utilitarian	ut = Utah il = Illinois	nd = North Dakota	hi = Hawaii
wind chill	wi = Wisconsin hi = Hawaii	in = Indiana il = Illinois	nd = North Dakota
Mohican	mo = Missouri ca = California	oh = Ohio	hi = Hawaii
misdemeanor	mi = Michigan me = Maine	sd = South Dakota or = Oregon	de = Delaware
compact disc	co = Colorado sc = South Carolina	pa = Pennsylvania	ct = Connecticut
new hymnbooks	ne = Nebraska ks = Kansas	mn = Minnesota	ok = Oklahoma
warm gaze	wa = Washington az = Arizona	ar = Arkansas	ga = Georgia

Extending the activity: Have groups of students suggest another word or phrase with several ZIP Code abbreviations for other groups to figure out. Have the students label the states on a United States map with the appropriate two letter abbreviation.

Seeing Stars

travelers who followed the star of Bethlehem	sea creature whose favorite food is mollusks	John Philip Sousa March
why Matt Dillon wore a star	a familiar symbol of Judaism	this rock group changed its name from *Airplane*
fort which inspired the Star-Spangled Banner	why cartoon characters sometimes have a group of start moving around their heads	color of a star given to a student for outstanding work
animated advertiser for Star-Kist tuna	their flag was known as the *Stars and Bars*	which way you turn a boat if you turn starboard
number of stars General Eisenhower wore after World War II	where the stars tonight are big and bright	name of the starship in *STAR TREK*™
a dark brown or glossy greenish-black bird	number of stars on a United States flag in 1958	city where entertainers are honored with stars on the sidewalk

Answers – Seeing Stars

the Wise Men	starfish	*The Stars and Stripes Forever*
he was the marshal of Dodge City, Kansas	the Star of David	Jefferson Starship
Fort McHenry, Maryland	they are concussed	gold star
Charlie the Tuna	Confederate States of America	to the right
five stars	deep in the heart of Texas	Enterprise
starling	48-Alaska and Hawaii became states in 1959	Hollywood, California and Buffalo, New York

Extending the activity: Share the story 'The Starfish Flinger' found at the Cherokee Focus website:

www.cherokeefocus.org/starfish.htm

Summary

Teachers can make more productive use of class time with appropriate use of sponge activities. Sponge activities can be useful for individuals, groups of students, and for the whole class. Such activities provide opportunities for practicing and extending what the students are learning. Collaboration and cooperation, group building, and thinking can be enhanced by using sponge activities.

Footnotes

[1] Hunter, R. (2004). *Madeline Hunter's Mastery Teaching: Increasing Instructional Effectiveness in Elementary and Secondary Schools.* Thousand Oaks, CA: Corwin, p. 117-119.

[2] Lyman, F., Jr. (1992). *Think-Pair-Share.* Washington, DC: National Education Association. (Videotape)

[3] Adapted from an activity by Foyle, H. C., & Lyman, L. (1991). A Sponge Activity to Spark Student Interest – Geography Find. *Geographic Insights.* Kansas Geographic Alliance, Kansas State University. *1*, (2).

[4] Adapted from an activity in *Cooperative Learning in the Elementary Classroom* (1993) by Lawrence Lyman, Harvey C. Foyle, & Tara C. Azwell. Washington, DC: National Education Association.

Chapter 10
Becoming the Teacher You Want to Be

'Would you tell me, please, which way I ought to go from here?'
'That depends a good deal on where you want to get to,' said the Cat.
'I don't much care where –', said Alice.
'Then it doesn't matter which way you go,' said the Cat.
'– so long as I get somewhere,' Alice added as an explanation.
'Oh, you're sure to do that,' said the Cat, 'if you only walk long enough.'

Alice and the Cheshire Cat
in *Alice in Wonderland* by Lewis Carroll

Successful teaching requires careful planning and requires a tremendous commitment of time and energy. Effective teachers make the best possible use of their available time, energy, and resources. For both beginning and experienced teachers, reaching their personal and professional goals can be both challenging and rewarding.

Reaching Personal and Professional Goals

Identify your personal and professional priorities
Invest the time and energy needed to give your personal best
Set reasonable goals with timetables
Communicate with family, friends, and colleagues
Demonstrate wellness and manage stress
Take time for reflection
Celebrate the efforts you make and the successes you earn

Much is expected of today's teachers. The most effective teachers are also effective human beings who have clear priorities, both personal and professional. They are able to cope with the many demands made of teachers because they know what they are doing and why they are doing it. They make choices which are consistent with their priorities.

Effective practitioners in any profession are those who invest their *time and energy* and give their personal best to their personal and professional pursuits. Teachers who give their personal best demonstrate enthusiasm, empathy for others, and a positive attitude toward their students and colleagues.

Successful teachers are involved in a continuous process of professional growth throughout their careers. They are able to set *goals for improvement* which are reasonable and to commit to achieving their goals. They are able to retain their excitement and zest for teaching because they are engaged in refining their teaching and in trying new ideas and strategies to become even more effective in the classroom.

Being able to balance their personal and professional lives is an important goal for teachers. Maintaining personal relationships by *communicating regularly with family and friends* is one of the most important ways to achieve this balance. Family and friends can help to provide support and encouragement which are essential to success and happiness.

Successful professionals also network regularly with colleagues, both personally and through virtual media. Colleagues who are positive and encouraging are often in the best position to understand the challenges and frustrations all teachers experience from time to time. They can often give perspective and encouragement which can help deal with the problems teachers inevitably encounter in working in today's schools.

Personal *wellness* is another important factor in reaching personal and professional goals. Wellness includes both emotional and physical wellness. The ability to manage personal and professional *stress* is an essential skill which is necessary to cope with pressures which can reduce the teacher's energy and effectiveness.[1]

Reflection and *celebration* are often neglected by busy professionals, but they are both very important to achieving goals, sustaining personal and professional relationships, managing stress, and finding fulfillment. **Reflection** involves taking time to assess how well things are going, what progress is being made toward personal and professional goals, and to plan for necessary adjustments and changes consistent with the teacher's personal and professional philosophy.

Celebration is recognizing the hard work that teachers put in for their students and being aware of how important those efforts are to the success of students. Effective teachers celebrate their own successes and recognize the efforts and successes of others.

"Reflection and Goal Setting"

Goal Setting Websites

Five Habits of Highly Effective Teachers
www.soyouwanttoteach.com/5-habits-of-highly-effective-teachers/

Setting personal goals
www.classroom-management-success.org/setting-personal-goals.html

Classroom goals
www.ndt-ed.org/TeachingResources/ClassroomTips/Goal_Setting.htm

Finding a Teaching Job

The career planning services offered by the college or university can help the prospective teacher build a placement file, create a resume, and gather the recommendations needed to apply for teaching positions. The following suggestions can also help with the process of *applying* for a teaching job and with the *job interview*.

1. Carefully select the school districts to which you send applications. Take the time to fill out application materials carefully and respond thoughtfully to any essay questions which may be a part of the application. Be sure to *proofread* your application and supporting materials for errors before submitting them.

2. When you are invited to an interview, do some *research* before the interview. Visit the web site of the district as well as any of the schools you know of that may have openings. Look for the district's mission statement and goals and be aware of general information about the district. This research will help you respond if you are asked why you are interested in working in the district and its schools.

3. Review your philosophy of teaching and the belief statements that were discussed in chapter 2. Be ready to explain your philosophy and beliefs about teaching *succinctly and clearly*. Be prepared to give *examples* from your internship experiences which support your beliefs. For example, if you state that you will work tirelessly to help all children be successful, be ready to tell about a student or two you worked with for whom you put forth extra effort.

4. Have a notebook of *lesson plans* and/or a *video example* of your teaching during your internship experiences to share at your interview if you are asked to do so. A teacher work sample completed during your internship can provide excellent documentation of your planning, teaching, and assessment decisions.

5. During the interview, *listen carefully* and *respond concisely* to the questions asked – usually no more than two or three sentences per question. If the interviewers want additional information, they will ask for it. Be prepared to respond to questions like these:

   a. Tell us a little bit about yourself.
   b. What is your philosophy of education?
   c. What are some experiences you have had in working with children?
   d. What grade levels or ages of students are you interested in working with?
   e. Why are you interested in working in our school district or school?
   f. What were some challenges you faced during your internship experiences?
   g. What classroom management strategies work well for you?
   h. What teaching strategies do you use to keep students actively engaged?
   i. How do you promote collaboration and cooperation among students?
   j. What skills do you have in working with technology in the classroom?
   k. How do you plan to involve family members of your students?
   l. What do you expect to be doing in five years?
   m. What are your weaknesses?
   n. What are your strengths?
   o. We have many qualified applicants for our teaching jobs. Why should we hire you?

6. The interviewers may ask if *you* have any questions for *them.* This is generally *not* the appropriate time to inquire about salary or benefits – this information will be provided to you at another time. You may want to ask about *one* of the following:

   a. opportunities for coaching or extracurricular assignments
   b. staff development opportunities in the school district
   c. partnerships the district may have with universities or educational cooperatives for graduate education
   d. community resources such as housing and recreation
   e. something the district is doing that you read about on their web site or in the materials they sent you

7. After the interview, send a note to the person who was in charge of the interviewing process thanking him or her for the opportunity to interview and expressing your interest and enthusiasm for teaching in the district.

8. Check back with the district to let them know you are still interested in a teaching position.

Edutopia: How to Find Your Dream Teaching Job
www.edutopia.org/school-employment-finding-teaching-job

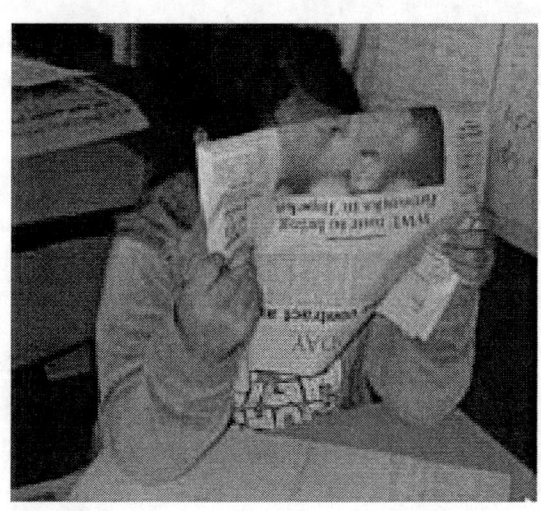

Getting Ready for Your New Classroom

After you accept a teaching position, you are ready to begin planning for a successful teaching experience in the specific context of your new district and school. Some suggestions for getting started:

1. Ask the district or school to send you *curriculum standards* for the school district for the grade level you will be teaching. *Teachers' editions* of textbooks used at the grade level may be helpful as well. It is important to identify the knowledge and skills which your students are expected to acquire.

2. Identify *connections* between the subject areas you are teaching. This can be helpful in constructing a long term plan for the school year. For example, if the students will be studying about weather, math skills might be connected to determine differences in temperatures and construct graphs. Map skills might be used to help students locate areas with different climate.

3. Review your *philosophy and beliefs* and think about writing a statement of those beliefs for your future students or family members (like the ones in chapter 2 of this book).

4. Think about the *first days of school* and do some planning to begin building your classroom community. Check out the school district resource center if they have one or the media center at your school for materials and resources.

5. Review the *rules and procedures* you plan to work on with your students to insure their safety, comfort, and productivity. You may want to share a draft of these rules and procedures with your administrator to get his or her feedback.

6. Don't plan *too much* for a specific grade level or school assignment – the grade level you are teaching or the school at which you may be teaching can sometimes change before the school year begins due to enrollment or other factors.

Arranging the Classroom for Safety and Productivity

The *physical arrangement* of your classroom is an important factor in helping your students to be successful. As soon as you know the classroom in which you will be teaching, look at the size of the room, furniture, and equipment that are available to you. You may want to visit other classrooms in the school to get ideas on how to arrange your room from teachers who teach in spaces similar to yours.

You will want to identify any additional furniture, equipment, or technology that would enhance your classroom. You can begin a wish list in the event funds become available. Grants may be available from the school district, Parent Teacher Organization, or external organizations for supplies, equipment, or remodeling.

In every classroom, there are some features such as windows and doors which are fixed. This will affect the way you arrange your classroom. There are many other factors that you will need to think about as you plan your classroom arrangement such as[2]:

1. Where will whole class instruction be presented? (location of the smart board and marker boards will affect this decision)

2. What areas or centers will I have for small group work? Where will these be located?

3. Will the desks or tables be arranged in rows or groups to start the school year?

4. Where will the classroom library and reading area, if any, be located?

5. Where will the students work with computers and other technology? (computer screens should be clearly visible to the teacher)

6. Where will the teacher desk be located? Where will teacher files and materials be stored?

7. Where will student 'mailboxes' be located for notes and returned work?

8. Where will students store coats, lunchboxes, and backpacks?

9. Where will students turn in work which they have completed?

10. Where will student work be displayed? (something from every student should always be on display in the classroom or in the hallway)

The teacher should evaluate the way the classroom is arranged on a regular basis to assure safety and productivity. Some suggestions:[3]

1. Always be sure that the teacher can see every student and be seen by every student in the room. Looks for corners, bookshelves, and other areas where students may be out of view.

2. The room arrangement should facilitate safe student movement. In the event of an emergency, students will be able to leave the room quickly and easily.

3. Floors are kept free of obstructions such as electrical cords which could trip students. Spills are cleaned up promptly according to safety guidelines.

4. Students have chairs and desks or tables which are appropriate for their physical size.

5. Students can see the smart board from where they are sitting.

6. Scissors, tools, glass, and hazardous materials are stored safely.

7. Perishable food is removed from the classroom at the end of the week or sooner.

8. Ventilation and lighting are appropriate. Problems are reported to the office.

9. Adequate containers or cages are provided for any pets in the classroom.

10. All electrical outlets and switches have appropriate covers.

Sample Classroom Floor Plans
www.learnnc.org/lp/pages/742

CLASSROOM ENVIRONMENT

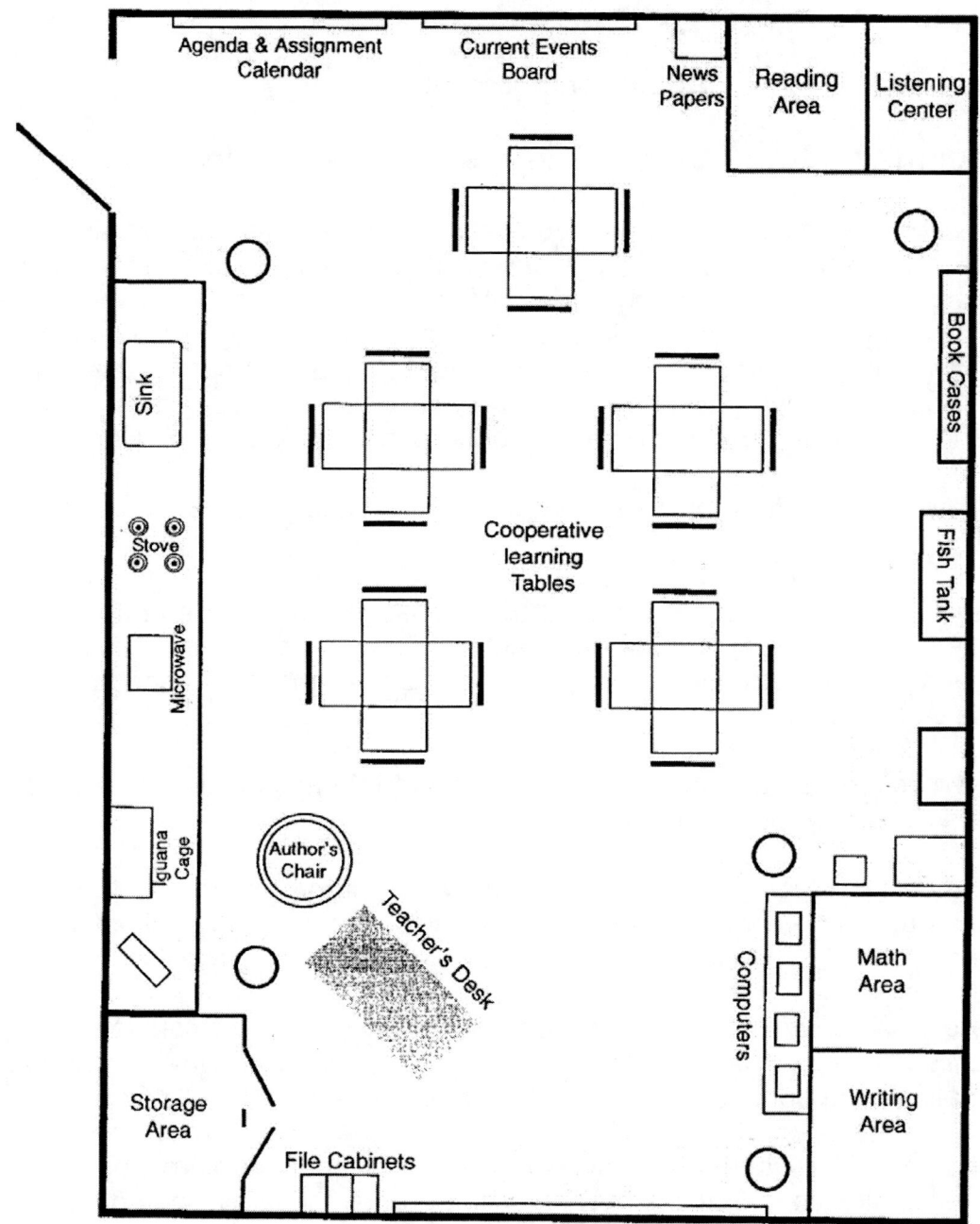

Adapted from Azwell, Foyle, Lyman, & Smith. (1999). *Constructing Curriculum in Context.* Kendall/Hunt Publishing Company, p. 545.

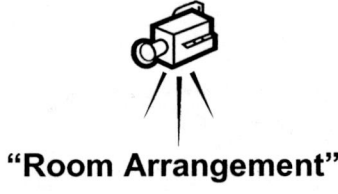

"Room Arrangement"

Grading and Reporting to Parents and Family Members

In chapter eight, the importance of communicating positively with parents and family members was discussed. As you begin working in a particular district and school setting, it is important to consider how you will develop appropriate standards for grading and reporting student progress to parents and their family members. Some factors which will influence your decisions about grading and reporting are: district expectations, your personal philosophy as a teacher, school standards, and the students you will be teaching. Some of the considerations to think about include[4]:

1. What are the specific grading procedures established by your district and school?

2. What information is found on the report card issued to parents and family members of students at your grade level? Remember, you will need to have *data and other information* to support your assessment of each of the criteria on the report card.

3. How will you keep parents and family members informed of their student's progress between report cards?

4. What meetings does the school schedule with parents (such as 'Back to School Night') where you will be providing information to parents about your grading system?

5. Is there a school web site where parents and family members can see their student's grades and missing assignments? Will you have grading information or student products on a class web site?

6. To what extent will students be involved in parent teacher conferences? Will they be constructing portfolios to share with parents and family members?

7. What is the policy of your school on academic dishonesty? How does academic dishonesty affect the student's grade?

8. What is the school policy on homework? How does homework affect the student's grade? Do parents and family members have access to a homework 'hotline' where they can check for their student's homework assignments by phone or online?

9. What tools will you use to keep student progress information organized and accurate?

10. If a grade is challenged by a parent or family member, what is the procedure for appeal?

Grading Systems
www.answers.com/topic/school-grading-systems

Becoming an Advocate for the Teaching Profession

The professional educator is an *advocate* for his or her profession. One of the most important ways to support the teaching profession is to *recognize and support* the efforts your colleagues, coworkers, and administrators are making in the school setting. Too often, hardworking teachers and others who work in the schools do not receive sufficient positive feedback about their efforts. As a colleague, you can support your fellow teachers, classified personnel at your school and your administrators through *informal interactions*[5] which:

1. *Show consideration* to let your colleagues know you like them and care about them.
   Examples:
   a. I know you were sick yesterday. Are you feeling better?
   b. How is your graduate class going?
   c. I heard your daughter won an award. Congratulations.
   d. How can I help?

2. *Share positive feedback* when you hear something positive from others.
   Examples:
   a. Mrs. Smith told me she is so glad that her son is in your class this year.
   b. The substitute told me how well your students behaved yesterday.
   c. Amy said you were her favorite teacher.

3. *Show appreciation* for your colleagues' efforts and hard work.
   Examples:
   a. What a terrific music program! You did a great job.
   b. The kids you had last year are doing so well on my fractions unit.
   c. I couldn't do it without you.

4. *Show respect* for your colleagues' experience and expertise.
   Examples:
   a. What do you think is the best way to teach this skill?
   b. Can you show me how to make this computer program work?
   c. How can I get through to John? Do you have any ideas?

Although these informal interactions with colleagues, coworkers, and administrators may seem simple, they contribute to a more positive school climate which benefits students as well as the adults in the school. Parents and family members also appreciate teachers who let them know their parenting efforts are recognized and who thank them for their support and help.

Positive Attitudes in the Workplace
www.self-improvement-advice.org/positive-attitude-in-the-workplace.html

It is also important to be an advocate for the teaching profession outside of the school setting. There has been a steady diet of negative information about schools and teachers since the release of the Nation at Risk Report in 1983. This has taken its toll on public confidence in education and on teacher morale. According to Paul Houston, executive director of the American Association of School Administrators, "That was the rising tide we got engulfed in – the rising tide of negative reports … after you've been knocked over for the 15th time and you're spitting up sand, you say, I want to go home."[6]

When visiting with family, friends, and neighbors, look for opportunities to tell about the good things happening in the schools, the hardworking teachers, and the progress that students are making. Writing a letter to the editor, attending school board meetings, and becoming informed about legislation that may affect schools are other important advocacy steps teachers can take. And, of course, all teachers have the responsibility to become informed and vote in local and national elections.

Managing Stress and Finding Balance

While teaching can be a wonderfully rewarding and fulfilling profession, today's teachers face many challenges and frustrations, many of which have been discussed in this book. It is important for all professionals to manage their stress levels and to find a balance between their professional and personal lives. Teachers who fail to deal effectively with the stresses in their lives can face health problems and professional burnout and may eventually leave the profession. Some suggestions for managing stress and finding balance[7]:

1. Maintain a healthy weight through appropriate diet and exercise.
2. Eliminate unhealthy habits such as tobacco use.
3. Get sufficient sleep and rest.
4. Use alcohol sparingly or not at all.
5. Have a regular physical examination.
6. Work a reasonable number of hours – do not allow work to dominate your life.
7. Have a hobby or interest outside of education.
8. Avoid talking only about school after hours.
9. Maintain relationships with family and friends who make you feel comfortable.
10. Have a sense of humor.
11. Be flexible.
12. Take one thing at a time.
13. Avoid competition with your colleagues, friends, and family.
14. Set realistic goals and work to achieve them.
15. Take positive action to deal with problems and concerns that cause you to worry.

Websites for additional information and ideas on managing stress and finding balance:

Mayo Clinic
www.mayoclinic.com/health/stress-management/MY00435

National Institute for Mental Health
www.nimh.nih.gov

The Importance of Professional Reflection

As you are working with your students, it is important to take time to *reflect* on your teaching on a regular basis. Do these elements exist in your classroom? If not, why not? What can you and your students do to make your class an even better place to be?

A   is for *approval*. Do your students receive regular messages of approval from their teacher and from their peers?

B   is for *best*. Do the students and the teacher give their personal best in class each day?

C   is for *connections*. Does the curriculum connect to the real lives, to the interests, and to the needs of the students?

D   is for *dreams*. What are your students' dreams? How can you work with your students to help their dreams become reality?

E   is for *empathy*. Do you take time to let students know that you care about them and support them in their struggles?

F   is for *fun*. What is being done to make learning fun and exciting?

G   is for *goals*. Do you help students set realistic goals for their academic, social, and behavioral growth and celebrate the *effort* they make to achieve these goals?

H   is for *haven*. Is the classroom a haven from the hopelessness, despair, and injustice too many students experience outside of school?

I   is for *instruction*. Do you use an appropriate variety of instructional strategies and media to facilitate student learning?

J   is for *joy*. Is your classroom a place of joy? Do you and the students want to come there each day?

K   is for *kindness*. Do you and your students treat each other as they would like to be treated?

L   is for *listening*. Do you and your students honestly try to listen to and understand each other?

M   is for *models*. What do you do to be a positive role model for students?

N   is for *niche*. Do you help all students find a special niche in the classroom? Do all students feel important and wanted in the classroom?

O   is for *opportunities*. Do all students have regular opportunities for success?

P   is for *patience*. Changing undesirable student behavior, inspiring students who are discouraged or burned out on school, and keeping students actively involved requires the teacher to be patient and committed. Change is a process, not an event.

Q   is for *questions*. Robert Kennedy was quoted as saying: "There are those who look at things the way they are and ask *why*? I dream of things that never were and ask *why not?*"[8] Do you encourage your students to ask challenging questions and to pursue the answers?

R   is for *respect*. Do you and your students demonstrate respect for each other?

S   is for *skills*. Are your students learning the skills they will need to be successful in life, such as managing conflict, getting along with others, and how to make friends?

T   is for *teamwork*? Do your students work together as a team to achieve common goals?

U   is for *understand*. Do students feel their teacher and their peers try to understand them?

V   is for *vistas*. Do you present a future consisting of limitless vistas and encourage students to try to reach them?

W   is for *welcome*. Do all students actually feel welcome in the classroom each day?

X   is for *Xerox*®. How can we expect students to be creative if they are asked to fill in the blanks on Xeroxed worksheets?

Y   is for "*yes, you can*". Do you say this more often than "no, you can't"?

Z   is for *zest*. Do you retain the sense of zest, excitement, and enthusiasm you had when you began teaching?

Celebration

Celebrating your hard work and your successes is an important factor in maintaining a positive attitude and enthusiasm for teaching and for dealing with stress. A crucial part of the reflection process is identifying the successful things you do as a teacher that work well for your students and help you to reach your goals. One strategy for celebration is to keep a journal in which you record one or two sentences a day about something positive that happened – a student who finally grasped an elusive concept, a random act of kindness performed by one of your students or a coworker, a word of thanks from a parent or family member. Taking time to read through your journal periodically can help you maintain a focus on the positive things that are going well and help to reduce stress and burnout.

"An Inspirational Teacher Quote Presentation"

Summary

To be able to make the many management decisions required in a busy classroom, the teacher must be willing to devote time and energy to teaching. Being able to set realistic and attainable personal and professional goals is an important part of a teacher's professional growth. As the teacher becomes more effective personally and professionally, his or her management decisions will usually become more effective as well.

As the teacher begins a new career or a new school year, important decisions need to be made before the students arrive. How will the room be arranged? What rules and procedures will help make the classroom safe and productive? What will be done during the first weeks of school to begin to create a classroom community that encourages collaboration and cooperation among students? What grading and reporting procedures will be used and what data will need to be collected?

In addition to supporting the academic and social needs of their students, teachers need to promote a positive school climate by interacting collegially with their coworkers and with the parents and the family members of their students. Outside of school, teachers need to be advocates for the teaching profession and the dedicated people who work with today's challenging students.

Teachers need to take the time to reflect on their teaching and to make adjustments as needed. An important part of the reflection process is celebrating the hard work and successes that are the results of the teacher's commitment of time and energy.

Success in teaching is a *journey,* not a destination. Classroom management will be a part of your journey throughout your teaching career. As you create safe and need fulfilling classroom communities for your students, you will make your journey through teaching meaningful and worthwhile.

Footnotes

[1] Lyman, L., Wilson, A. P., Garhart, C. K., Heim, M. O., & Winn, W. O. (1987). *Clinical Instruction and Supervision for Accountability* (2nd ed.). Dubuque, IA: Kendall/Hunt, p. 67-68.

[2] Azwell, T. S., Foyle, H.C., Lyman, L., & Smith, N. L. (1999). *Constructing Curriculum in Context.* Dubuque, IA: Kendall/Hunt, p. 520-521.

[3] Adapted from a list in Lyman, L., Wilson, A. P., Garhiart, C. K., Heim, M. O., & Winn, W. O., p. 95-96.

[4] Adapted from Azwell et. al. p. 525-526.

[5] Adapted from Lyman, L., & Foyle, H. C. (1990). *Cooperative Grouping for Interactive Learning: Students, Teachers, and Administrators.* Washington, DC: National Education Association, p. 25-26.

[6] Toppo, G. (2008). 'Nation at Risk: The Best or the Worst Thing for Education?' in www.usatoday.com/news/education/2008-04-22-nation-at-risk_N.htm Retrieved Dec. 28, 2010.

[7] Adapted from Lyman, L., Wilson, A. P., Garhart, C. K., Heim, M. O., & Winn, W., p. 68-69.

[8] Kennedy, R. F. quoted at http://thinkexist.com/quotes/robert_francis_kennedy.

Afterword

The authors have repeated the idea several times in this publication that classroom management is not a *destination* a teacher arrives at, but rather a *journey* that continues throughout the teacher's career. As you continue your journey, please remember the following key concepts.

1. ***Relationships*** are the key to effective teaching. Your relationships with your students, parents and family members, and colleagues are one of the most important factors in determining how much effort your students will put forth to learn, how your students will treat each other and you, and how your classroom community will function. Building trust is a vital part of building and maintaining positive relationships. This publication was enhanced by photos and video clips from actual classrooms. The authors are deeply indebted to our colleagues and friends who trusted us and permitted us to come into their classrooms for ideas and visual images to share with you.

2. ***Connections*** help to make learning easier and more meaningful for your students. In addition to photos from classrooms, you saw throughout this publication pictures of our family members, including spouses, children and grandchildren, pets, and places we have visited. Each teacher brings pieces of his or her own culture and experiences into the classroom as the authors did in this publication. Magic takes place when teachers connect their own cultures and experiences with the unique cultures and experiences of their students. Our students can teach us so much about becoming effective teachers.

3. ***Creativity*** is important. There is no single formula, program, or strategy for becoming an effective teacher. The best teachers find creative ways to make the curriculum come alive for their students, to meet the needs of students who are struggling, and to build and nurture a caring and productive classroom community. For example, a character like Zardozz can come to class on special days to build interest and nurture class culture. As a teacher, you will have many creative ideas which will make your classroom an exciting place to be.

As you continue your journey as a teacher, it is important to ask yourself, on a regular basis, *if I were a student in the class I am teaching, would I be a happy and productive member of this classroom community?* Our journey also continues and we look forward to sharing new ideas and updates with you on the website associated with this publication.

Larry Lyman   ***Harvey Foyle***   ***Allyson Lyman***

Appendix A

Bibliography

Albert, L. (2003). *Cooperative discipline: Teacher's handbook.* Circle Pines, MN: American Guidance Service.

Armstrong, T. (2009). *Multiple intelligences in the classroom* (3rd ed.). Alexandria, VA: Association for Supervision and Curriculum Development.

Aronson, E., & Patnoe, S. (1997). *The jigsaw classroom* (2nd ed.). New York, NY: Longman.

Azwell, T. S., Foyle, H. C., Lyman, L., & Smith, N. L. (1999). *Constructing curriculum in context.* Dubuque, IA: Kendall/Hunt.

Blanchard, K. (2002). *Whale done! The power of positive relationships.* New York, NY: The Free Press.

Bluestein, J. (2007). *The win-win classroom.* Thousand Oaks, CA: Corwin.

Burke, K. (2008). *What to do with the kid who ...: Developing cooperation, self-discipline, and responsibility in the classroom* (3rd ed.). Thousand Oaks, CA: Corwin.

Cangelosi, J. S. (2007). *Classroom management strategies: Gaining and maintaining students' cooperation.* Hoboken, NJ: John Wiley & Sons.

Charles, C. M., & Senter, G. W. (2008). *Elementary classroom management* (5th ed.). Upper Saddle River NJ: Allyn and Bacon.

Coloroso, B. (2008). *Just because it's not wrong doesn't make it right: From toddlers to teens, teaching kids to think and act ethically.* New York, NY: Penguin.

Covey, S. R. (1989). *The seven habits of highly effective people.* New York, NY: Simon and Schuster.

Curwin, R. L., Mendler, A. N., & Mendler, B. D. (2008). *Discipline with dignity: New challenges, new solutions.* Alexandria, VA: Association for Supervision and Curriculum Development.

Davis, S., & Davis, J. (2007). *Schools where everyone belongs: Practical strategies for reducing bullying.* Champaign, IL: Research Press.

Delpit, L. (1995). *Other people's children: Cultural conflict in the classroom.* New York, NY: The New Press.

Dishon, D., & O'Leary, P. W. (1998). *A guidebook for cooperative learning: A technique for creating more effective schools* (2nd ed.). Holmes Beach FL: Learning Publications.

Evertson, C. M., & Emmer, E. T. (2009). *Classroom management for elementary teachers* (8th ed.). Upper Saddle River, NJ: Allyn and Bacon.

Foyle, H. C., & Lyman, L. (2007). *Cooperative learning: Engaging students.* DVD. Scotts Valley, CA: Create Space.

Foyle, H. C., & Lyman, L. (2007). *Cooperative learning: Grouping for interactive learning.* DVD. Scotts Valley, CA: Create Space.

Foyle, H. C., Lyman, L., & Thies, S. A. (1991). *Cooperative learning in the early childhood classroom.* Washington, DC: National Education Association.

Foyle, H. C. (editor, 1995). *Interactive learning in the higher education classroom: cooperative, collaborative, and active learning strategies.* Washington, DC: National Education Association.

Gardner, H. (2006). *Multiple intelligences: New horizons in theory and practice.* New York, NY: Basic Books.

Gibbs, J., & Ronzone, P. (2006). *Reaching all by creating tribes learning communities.* Windsor, CA: Center Source Systems.

Ginsberg, M. B., & Wlodkowski, R. J. (2000). *Creating highly motivating classrooms for all students: A schoolwide approach to powerful teaching with diverse learners.* San Francisco: Jossey-Bass.

Glasser, W. (1998). *Choice theory: A new psychology of personal freedom.* New York, NY: HarperCollins.

Glasser, W. (1988). *Choice theory in the classroom.* New York, NY: HarperCollins.

Goleman, D. P. (2006). *Social intelligence: The new science of human relationships.* New York, NY: Bantam Books.

Harmin, M., & Toth, M. (2006). *Inspiring active learning: A complete handbook for today's teachers.* Alexandria, VA: Association for Supervision and Curriculum Development.

Hunter, M. (1990). *Discipline that develops self-discipline.* Thousand Oaks, CA: Corwin.

Jensen, E. (2008). *Enriching the brain: How to maximize every learner's potential.* San Francisco: Jossey-Bass.

Johnson, D., & Johnson, R. (1998). *Learning together and alone: Cooperative, competitive, and individualistic* learning (5th ed.). Alexandria, VA: Association for Supervision and Curriculum Development.

Kagan, S. (1994). *Cooperative learning.* San Clemente, CA: Kagan Cooperative Learning.

Kohn, A. (2006). *Beyond discipline: From compliance to community.* Alexandria, VA: Association for Supervision and Curriculum Development.

Kottler, J. A., & Kottler, E. (2009). *Students who drive you crazy: Succeeding with resistant, unmotivated, and otherwise difficult young people* (2nd ed.). Thousand Oaks, CA: Corwin.

Larrivee, B. (2009). *Authentic classroom management: Creating a learning community and building reflective practice* (3rd ed.). Upper Saddle River, NJ: Merrill.

Lyman, L., & Foyle, H. C. (1990). "The Constitution in action: A cooperative learning approach" in *Georgia Social Science Journal.* Spring, 1990. *21*(1), 24-34.

Lyman, L., & Foyle, H. C. (1990). *Cooperative grouping for interactive learning: Students, teachers, and administrators.* Washington, DC: National Education Association.

Lyman, L., Foyle, H. C., & Azwell, T. S. (1993). *Cooperative learning in the elementary classroom.* Washington, DC: National Education Association.

Lyman, L., & Foyle, H. C. (1998). Facilitating collaboration in schools. *Teaching and Change.* Spring-Summer, 1998. *5*(3-4), 312-339.

Lyman, L., & Foyle, H. C. (2010). Group building for improved instruction in postsecondary social science classrooms. *National Social Science Journal. 33*(2), 116-120.

Lyman, L., & Foyle, H. C. (1991). Teaching geography using cooperative learning. *Journal of Geography.* September-October, 1991. *90*(5), 223-226.

Lyman, L., Wilson, A. P., Garhart, C. K., Heim, M. O., & Winn, W. O. (1987). *Clinical instruction and supervision for accountability* (2nd ed.). Dubuque, IA: Kendall/Hunt.

McCourt, F. (2005). *Teacher man.* New York, NY: Scribner.

Meier, D. (1995). *The power of their ideas: Lessons for America from a small school in Harlem.* Boston: Beacon Press.

Morehead, M. A., Lyman, L., & Foyle, H.C. (2009). *Working with student teachers: Getting and giving the best* (2nd ed.). Lanham, MD: Rowman and Littlefield.

Nelsen, J., Lott, L., & Glenn, H. S. (1993). *Positive discipline in the classroom.* Rocklin, CA: Prima Publishing.

Payne, R. (2006). *Working with students: Discipline strategies for the classroom.* Highland, TX: aha! Process.

Peterson, R. (1992). *Life in a crowded place: Making a learning community.* Portsmouth, NH: Heinemann.

Reider, B. (2005). *Teach more and discipline less: Preventing problem behaviors in the K-6 classroom.* Thousand Oaks, CA: Corwin.

Sapon-Shevin, M. (2010). *Because we can change the world: A practical guide to building cooperative, inclusive classroom communities* (2nd ed.). Thousand Oaks, CA: Corwin.

Weinstein, C. S., & Mignano, A. J., Jr. (2007). *Elementary classroom management: Lessons from research and* practice (4th ed.). Boston: McGraw-Hill.

Wong, H. K., & Wong, R. T. (2009). *The first days of school: How to be an effective teacher.* Mountain View, CA: Harry K. Wong Publications.

Appendix B
Chapter Questions

Chapter One
Teaching Today's Students

1. Read the paper on classroom management prepared by the National Education Association. www.nea.org/assets/docs/mf_cmbrief.pdf Which *five* of the practices recommended in the paper will be the *most important* for you as a beginning teacher in your future classroom? Please give a reason for each idea you choose.

2. What are some of the *challenges* you will find in today's classrooms? List *three* things you learned while reading this chapter that will help you meet these challenges and give a reason why each of the things you chose is important.

3. Why is it important for a teacher to create a *caring* environment in the classroom?

4. Why is it important for students to have opportunities to hear *different ideas* and *points of view* in the classroom?

5. How can teachers help their students to be prepared for the inevitable *changes* that will take place in the future?

6. How can teachers help to make learning *meaningful* for their students?

Chapter Two
Structuring the Interactive Classroom

1. Besides a safe and orderly environment, what are three *correlates of Effective Schools* identified by Ron Edmonds and Larry Lezotte?

2. What are two examples of *high risk* student activities which require even more careful supervision by the teacher than when students are working in the classroom?

3. Look at "Suggestions for Working with At-Risk Students", "Suggestions for Ways for Helping Students to Feel Successful" (link), and "Designing Learning Activities for Student Success" in the chapter. What are *five ideas* that you could use in your PDS classrooms when you are working with students?

4. What are three things will you do to make your future classroom *physically and emotionally safe* for your students?

5. What are three things you will do to help students *to belong and to be accepted* in your future classroom?

6. What are three things you will do to help students have some appropriate *power* and *to be recognized* in your future classroom?

7. What are three things you will do to help students have appropriate *freedom* in your future classroom?

8. What are three things you will do to help students *have fun* and *enjoy learning* in your future classroom?

9. What are three things you will do to provide appropriate *feedback* to students in your future classroom?

10. What are three things you will do to help all students be *successful* in your future classroom?

Chapter Three
Managing the Interactive Classroom

1. What is the *purpose* of rules and procedures in the classroom?

2. Why is it important for the teacher to *model* the rules and procedures?

3. At the beginning of the year, how can you get students to commit to following the class rules and procedures?

4. Why is it important to have a *signal* for stopping work and listening to the teacher?

5. What procedures does Sheila Broyles (link) use with her kindergarteners to prevent *problems in line*?

6. Why is *extinction* sometimes an appropriate way to deal with minor misbehavior?

7. What is the difference between *positive reinforcement* and *positive feedback*? Which is more powerful? Why?

8. What questions should the teacher ask himself or herself when *chronic misbehavior* occurs with a student or students?

9. What is *serious misbehavior*? What does the teacher need to do when serious misbehavior occurs?

10. How can *bystanders* help prevent and deal with bullying?

Chapter Four
Creating the Classroom Community –
The Group Building Process

1. What are some characteristics of *caring and productive* classroom communities?

2. Why are *group building activities* needed to build and sustain a classroom community?

3. What are the *benefits* of using group building activities with students?

4. What are the *components* of the group building process?

5. Where could a teacher locate possible *ideas and activities* to use in the group building process?

6. Read the material at one of the links provided for information on *copyright*. List three ideas about copyright laws and regulations that you need to remember as a teacher.

7. Howard Gardner has identified nine kinds of *multiple intelligences*. Which two multiple intelligences are particular strengths of yours? How will these strengths be useful in your classroom?

8. How does *observing student interaction* as students are working on group building activities help the teacher?

9. How can family members be involved in the group building process?

Chapter Five
Maintaining and Enhancing the Classroom Community

1. How do *rituals and traditions* promote a classroom community? What are two rituals or traditions from the list provided that you think you would like to incorporate in your own classroom?

2. Why should *special days* be celebrated more often in classrooms?

3. After group building activities have been used at the beginning of the year, what does the teacher need to do to *maintain* the classroom community?

4. What are possible ways to deal with *conflict* which will occur in the classroom?

5. What are some *causes* of conflict in the classroom?

6. Why is it beneficial for the teacher to anticipate how conflicts might occur in activities, programs, or other situations?

7. How can *class projects* enhance a classroom community?

Chapter Six
Using Collaborative and Cooperative Learning

1. When can a teacher productively use *collaborative* and *cooperative* learning activities in the classroom?

2. What *conditions* are necessary in order to successfully implement collaborative and cooperative learning?

3. Why should the teacher avoid using *group grading* in the classroom?

4. What are the *components* of collaborative and cooperative activities?

5. What are some possible *roles* for students that could be used in collaborative or cooperative activities? Why is it helpful to use roles?

6. What are some disadvantages of using *collaborative* groups instead of *cooperative* groups?

7. What are some *benefits*, proven by research, of using cooperative learning activities?

8. Why do teachers need to teach *social skills* and *communication skills* in order for students to be able to collaborate and cooperate successfully?

9. What are some ways for the teacher to *assess* cooperative learning activities?

10. What are some ways the teacher can help to make collaborative and cooperative learning successful in his or her classroom?

Chapter Seven
Activities for Collaborative and Cooperative Lessons

1. What steps should the teacher consider when *planning* a cooperative learning lesson?

2. What are some *group skills* that the teacher can have the students work on during cooperative learning activities?

3. How can the use of *technology* enhance cooperative learning activities?

4. What is the *Teams-Games-Tournaments* strategy? How could you use it in your future classroom?

5. How can the teacher *extend* a cooperative learning activity?

6. According to the chapter summary, what steps need to be a part of *every* cooperative learning lesson plan?

Chapter Eight
Promoting Active Involvement

1. Why is *Dreikurs'* theory of student's *goals* for misbehavior useful to teachers?

2. What four interruptions to the *smoothness* and *momentum* of a lesson did *Kounin* identify? Why is this important for teachers to keep in mind while they are teaching?

3. Why is *positive feedback* more useful than *positive reinforcement*?

4. Why are *rhetorical questions* and *sarcasm* ineffective when teachers are communicating with their students?

5. What do teachers need to do to listen *empathically* to their students?

6. How can *class meetings* be useful in the classroom?

7. How can teachers communicate effectively with *parents* and *family members*?

8. How can teachers make the best use of the time available for *conferences* with parents and family members?

9. Why is it important for the teacher to *check for student understanding* when teaching? What are some ways to do this?

Chapter Nine
Activities to Use Classroom Time Productively

1. What is a *sponge activity*?

2. How could you use sponge activities in your classroom?

3. Where can you find *ideas and resources* for sponge activities?

4. What kinds of groups and organizations have *websites* that you could use to locate ideas to use for sponge activities?

Chapter Ten
Becoming the Teacher You Want to Be

1. Why is it important for teachers to set *improvement goals*?

2. What three suggestions for *finding a teaching job* did you find most helpful? Give a reason for each suggestion you choose.

3. What three suggestions for *arranging your future classroom* did you think were the most important to remember? Give a reason for each suggestion you choose.

4. What ideas for becoming an *advocate for the teaching profession* are discussed in this chapter?

5. Why do teachers need to work on strategies for managing *stress*?

6. Why is it important for teachers to *celebrate* their hard work and successes?

Appendix C

Learning Activities

Activity # 1 (Chapter 1)

1. Think back to *your own experiences* as a student in *elementary school.* Make a list of the rewards you remember which were used by *your* elementary teachers to encourage good behavior and achievement in school and make a list of consequences for misbehavior which your teachers used.

    Rewards   **Consequences**

2. Which of the *rewards* your teachers used, if any, did you like best?

3. Which of the *consequences*, if any, were you most afraid of?

4. Think back to *your own experiences* as a student in *elementary school.* Make a list of the rewards you remember which were used by *your* parents to encourage good behavior and achievement at home and in school and make a list of consequences for misbehavior at home and school which your parents used with *you*.

    Rewards   **Consequences**

5. Which of the *rewards* your parents used, if any, did you like best?

6. Which of the *consequences* your parents used, if any, were you most afraid of?

7. As a *future teacher,* make a list of the *rewards* you expect to receive by being a teacher and what you think will be the most difficult *challenges* you will face as a future teacher.

    Rewards   **Challenges**

Activity # 2 (Chapter 1)

Identify the domain *(cognitive, affective, psychomotor, or interpersonal)* to which each of these classroom management decisions belongs.

Classroom Management Decision	Domain
example Sending a copy of the classroom rules to family members and to the administrator	Cognitive
Making sure each student has something displayed in the classroom	
Planning time at the beginning of the year for students to get to know each other	
Having a class meeting when some students' feelings are hurt by teasing	
Checking student records to identify students with health concerns such as allergies	
Having students get up and stretch when they become restless during a lesson	
Visiting in private with a student who has been interrupting so she won't be embarrassed in front of the other students	
Modeling the correct use of playground equipment at the beginning of the school year	
Keeping a record of problems and concerns you have about the behavior of individual students	
Having students work together in heterogeneous groups to practice their math facts	
Making sure the student desks are arranged so that there is sufficient space for students to walk around safely	

Activity # 3 (Chapter 2)

There are several examples of promises or commitment statements in this chapter two. Create a *promise or commitment statement* which represents your philosophy and goals for your students. Your audience may be your future students, your future parents and family members, or school administrators who will interview you for a teaching position. Please identify the audience you are choosing at the beginning of your statement. You should be creative in constructing a promise or commitment statement that represents *you*. You may include graphics or illustrations if you choose. Your statement should not exceed two pages.

Activity # 4 (Chapter 3)

Read the following case studies and respond to the questions.

> *Abby is a student in your class who is frequently out of her seat and wandering around while the rest of the class is working at their seats.*

1. What *additional information* would be helpful to help you decide what to do?

2. What is the *first* thing you would try to deal with this behavior?

3. If the first thing you tried did not work, what would you do *next*?

4. If the first two things you tried did not work, what would you do *next*?

> *Ron is a student in your class who loves to read. He gets so involved in the stories he is reading that he often fails to complete his work on time.*

5. What is the *first* thing you would try to deal with this behavior?

6. If the first thing you tried did not work, what would you do *next*?

7. If the first two things you tried did not work, what would you do *next*?

> *Another one of your students, Carmen, is frequently late to school in the morning.*

8. Write an *I-message* you could use to let Carmen know you are concerned about her tardiness.

Activity # 5 (Chapter 4)

Locate an activity that you could use as a *group building activity* for the age group you are most interested in working with. You may use websites, books or magazines, an activity you have done or seen done in another setting, or an activity you create on your own. On the assigned date, you should bring *four* copies of the activity to class (three to share with others in your assigned group, one to turn in to the instructor).

Title of the Group Building Activity

Grade Level

Objective of the Activity

Materials Needed

Procedure

Individual Accountability

Source for the Group Building Activity

Activity # 6 (Chapter 8)

For examples 1-6, tell what the *student's goal* is (according to Dreikurs) and how you know.

1. During a lesson you are teaching on the dangers of tobacco use, Luis tells the class that his brother smokes all the time and you don't know what you're talking about.

2. You are wearing new pants that several colleagues have told you are very attractive. Sydney says loudly to the class that you "really look stupid in those ugly pants".

3. You ask the students to give you an example of a mammal. Cliff raises his hand and when you call on him, he answers, "I'm going to be an owl for Halloween this year."

4. Bob has not completed most of the assignment when the rest of the class has finished. You ask him why and he tells you he broke his pencil fifteen minutes ago.

5. Amy is reading aloud to herself when the students are supposed to be reading quietly.

6. After you give the students an assignment, Wendy announces, "I'm not going to do that. It's just more busy work."

For examples 7-10, tell whether the example is a *flip-flop*, a *dangle*, a *thrust,* or *stimulus bound* divergence (according to Kounin).

7. During a lesson on the Panama Canal, the teacher tells the class, "This reminds me of a trip we took to Venice when I was in college."

8. The teacher tells the class, "Oh, we forgot to finish the math assignment. Put your science books away and we will finish science later."

9. During a discussion on the American pioneers, the teacher comments to the class, "I wonder why the custodian is mowing today when the grass is still wet from that storm we had."

10. The teacher tells the class, "We'll come back to this later. Let's talk about the field trip we will be taking next week."

Activity # 7 (Chapter 8)

Read the following letter from a fourth grade teacher to the parents or guardians of her students. What *changes* would you make in the letter? Please give a reason for each change you would make. Each correct change is worth 2 points. Total available points = 10 points.

Dear Parents of 4th Grade Students,

Communication is the key to a successful relationship between school and home. During the first few weeks of school, I will be working on comprehending expository text, estimating numbers, basic math facts, systems of the human body, and geography. The students will be doing a lot of creative writing using the Six Trait model.

If your child is absent, please send a note on his return stating the reason for his absence. If you know he will be absent in advance, please send a note so he can obtain his homework.

If your child receives a D or F on an assignment or fails to turn in an assignment, he will be required to take the assignment or assignment information home and get a parent's signeture on it and return it to school on the following day. He will be required to redo or complete the assignment successfully. If the child fails to return a paper with the required signeture, the parent will be called the following morning to be informed of the problem.

I will send a note home if there is a problem with your child's behavior or attitude and your child will be required to return the note to school the next day with your signeture. If the child fails to return a behavior note, the parent will be called the following morning to be informed of the problem.

I hope you will be able to attend Back to School night so you can learn more about my class and my expectations. Please feel free to contact me with any question or concern before or after school.

Sincerely,

Ms. H. O. Stone
Fourth Grade Teacher

Activity # 8 (Chapter 9)

Find a website which has activities you could use for *sponge activities* with your Block 2 and Block 3 students and in your own classroom.

Write the following information on a sheet of paper and turn it in on the due date.

Your name

Website Name

URL

Date you accessed the web site

What kind of activities are available (one or two sentences only)

Activity # 9 (Chapter 10)

Choose any *five* questions from the list of possible *interview questions* in chapter 10. Tell how you would respond to each of the questions you choose if you were asked the question during an actual interview for a teaching position. Your response should not be longer than four sentences.

Activity # 10 (Chapter 10)

The National Institute of Mental Health and the Mayo Clinic provide the following suggestions for how to cope with stress. **Rate yourself on each of the suggestions.**

This is activity is for your information and reflection only – you will not turn it in.

Stress Reducing Activity	I currently do this.	Do not do, I need to start.	Do not do, I don't need to.
Work off stress by physical activity such as running, playing tennis, taking a walk, or gardening.			
Share worries and frustrations with someone your trust and respect such as a friend, family member, teacher, or clergyman.			
Get enough sleep and rest – most people need seven or eight hours of sleep every night.			
Avoid self-medication with alcohol and drugs which can hide symptoms of stress.			
Balance work and play – schedule regular times for activities which relax you.			
Set priorities and plan ahead to meet deadlines and expectations. Don't leave things until the last minute.			
Seek professional assistance from a counselor or other mental health professional if stress becomes overwhelming.			

Emporia State Counseling Center – 211 South Morse Hall (341-5221)

The staff of the Emporia State University Counseling Center are here to help you maintain a balanced and healthy life and succeed at ESU. Our range of services include counseling, art therapy, drug and alcohol prevention and referral, information and programs of interest to women and men, sexual assault prevention, and stress and anxiety management through biofeedback training.   www.emporia.edu/counseling/

Appendix D

Classroom Context Assignment

DESCRIPTION OF TEACHING CONTEXT

This context assignment was developed for use in Professional Development School classrooms as a requirement for the elementary and middle school Classroom Management course at Emporia State University by the course instructor, Lawrence Lyman. It can be adapted to other settings for teachers, interns, and student teachers who are observing students at the beginning of the school year.

Intern _____   District _____

School _____   Mentor Teacher _____

I. School Context (This information will be completed after meeting with the building principal.)

   A. What grade levels are found in this school? What special programs, if any, are found in this school?

   B. How many students are enrolled in the school? Do any students who are primarily schooled at home attend the school on a part-time basis?

   C. List the school administrator(s), secretary, custodian(s), and counselor assigned to this school. How long has the principal been at this particular school?

   D. What is the socioeconomic status of students attending this school? Does the school qualify for Title I assistance? What special grants does the school have for this school year?

   E. What is the ethnicity of students attending this school? (List approximate percentages)

Ethnicity	*Male*	*Female*	*Total*	*Percentage*
Asian				
Black				
Hispanic				
White				
Native American				
Unknown				
Total				

F. What is the approximate mobility rate of students in this school?

G. Does this school participate in Quality Performance Assessment or North Central Association of Schools and Colleges to meet Kansas state requirements for school accreditation?

H. List the target area goals from the School Improvement Plan which are being worked on.

I. List the faculty members responsible for the accreditation teams and each target area goal. (chairpersons only)

J. Briefly list the major activities that will take place related to school improvement at this particular school during this school year.

K. List the year school was built and the year(s) in which any addition(s) were added to the school.

L. List any unique or special features of this school.

II. Classroom Context

A. Draw a diagram of the classroom arrangement or take photographs of the classroom and include with this assignment.

B. How many desks, tables, and chairs are found in the classroom? Does the classroom feel crowded, adequate, or roomy?

C. How is the ventilation in the classroom? Does the classroom temperature seem too hot or cold? Are windows found in the room?

D. Are the acoustics of the classroom good? Do noises from outside the classroom interrupt and distract teacher and students?

E. How many bulletin boards are located in the classroom? How many are available outside the classroom (if any)? Is there work from every student in the class displayed on one or more of the bulletin boards?

F. What technology is available in the classroom? What technological resources do students have access to in other parts of the school? How often do they have access to these resources?

G. Describe any special or unique features of this classroom.

III. Human Resources

   A. Briefly describe your mentor teacher's professional background. (college degrees, special training, years of experience, previous experience supervising interns)

   B. List all adults (teachers, support personnel, etc.) with whom *all* students in the class work and tell how often all students work with each adult.

   C. List all adults with whom *one or more* of the students work and tell how often one or more students work with these adults.

   D. List all paraprofessionals, aides, and volunteers who work in your classroom on a regular basis and tell how often they are available.

   E. List all students who come from other classrooms to help in your classroom (if any) and tell how often they come.

IV. Students – *Do not list the names of the students.* Use a letter or number code or student initials as your mentor teacher prefers.

   A. How many students in your class participate in supplementary instructional programs such as Title 1, gifted education, learning resource, speech, or others? List each program in which there are students in each program. (Example = Title I reading - 3 students)

   B. List the major ethnic groups below and tally how many of each group is in your classroom.

   C. List the kinds of family structures below and tally how many of each group is in your classroom.

   Student lives with both parents –
   Student lives with mother –
   Student lives with father –
   Student lives with someone else –
   Other or unknown –

   D. Which students appear to be leaders in this classroom? How do you know?

   E. Which students appear to by shy or reticent in this classroom? How do you know?

   F. Which students appear to have difficulty getting along with other students? How do you know?

G. Which students appear to be achieving above grade level? How do you know?

H. Which students appear to be achieving at grade level? How do you know?

I. Which students appear to be achieving at below grade level? How do you know?

J. Which students need extra help to understand and participate in class activities? All the time or only in certain subjects? What do these students do when they become frustrated?

K. Which students appear to be socially skilled in the classroom? How do you know?

L. Which students appear to need more attention (either positive or negative) from the teacher other than other students? What do these students do to try to get the attention they want? What do they do when they do not get the attention they want?

M. Which students speak languages other than English?

N. List the students who appear to learn best when the following multiple intelligences are used:

    Verbal/Linguistic (Words)
    Logical/Mathematical (Numbers)
    Visual/Spatial (Pictures)
    Bodily/Kinesthetic (Movement)
    Musical/Rhythmic (Music)
    Interpersonal (People)
    Intrapersonal (Self)
    Natural (Nature)

O. Briefly discuss any special or unique characteristics of students in this classroom, which you have not mentioned above.

V. Classroom Structure

    A. List the rules of the classroom.

    B. List the consequences for breaking the rules in the classroom.

    C. List ways the teacher positively reinforces students who are behaving appropriately.

    D. List ways the teacher uses to keep students on task while he or she is teaching.

    E. List procedures for emergency drills and for crisis management in the classroom.

    F. Briefly discuss your understanding of your role as an intern in classroom management.

About the Authors

Lawrence Lyman is Professor and Professional Development School Coordinator in the Department of Early Childhood/Elementary Teacher Education at Emporia State University. He has been an elementary school teacher, elementary school principal, and university department chairperson. His doctorate in educational administration is from Kansas State University.

Harvey C. Foyle is Professor in the Department of Instructional Design and Technology at Emporia State University. He has been a secondary social studies teacher and a high school department chairperson. At the college and university level, he has taught history, political science, social sciences methods, teacher education, and technology education. His doctorate in curriculum and instruction is from Kansas State University.

Allyson L. Lyman is a fifth grade teacher in the Emporia Public Schools, Emporia, Kansas. She is a graduate of the nationally recognized elementary education program at Emporia State University where she completed internships in the Professional Development School program. She received a master's degree in Educational Leadership from Emporia State University and serves as a mentor teacher for Professional School interns.

Photos courtesy of Emporia State University (KS) and USD #253 Emporia (KS).